Out of print
13/7/1996.

£13.92

Feb 91.

Food Safety
A Practical Guide to the 1990 Act
by Teresa Hitchcock, MIEH, LL.B.

London
Fourmat Publishing
1990

ISBN 1 85190 115 9

First published 1990

Printed in Great Britain by
Billing & Sons Ltd, Worcester

© 1990 T. C. Hitchcock

Published by Fourmat Publishing,
133 Upper Street, Islington, London N1 1QP

Contents

Table of cases

Chapter 1

Introduction

In the eighteen months preceding the introduction of the Food Safety Bill there was a great amount of media attention focused upon the food bought by the consumer. Recent years have seen an alarming rise in the recorded incidence of food poisoning, with the figures for 1988 showing a threefold increase since 1982. Recorded cases are only the tip of the iceberg — gross under-reporting of incidents almost certainly exists. There have been many food hazard warnings issued by Government departments. Scientific evidence has illustrated the need to impose closer control over areas of the food industry and advanced food processing techniques have outgrown the present legislative controls.

The first publicly aired problem regarding unsafe food — the crisis over salmonella in eggs — was in 1988. This was followed by a series of scares about food contamination: an outbreak of botulism; a rare form of food poisoning caused by contaminated hazelnut yoghurt; and the discovery of listeria monocytogenes in a variety of foods. The arousal of public concern and awareness concerning such food issues has been further instanced by the vast increase in consumer complaints made to Environmental Health and Trading Standards Departments in recent months.

New, more forceful legislation has long been awaited. The 1984 Food Act was little more than a consolidating statute with an archaic and unwieldy legal framework which had its roots deeply entrenched in the early nineteenth century.

1. Historical development of food law

Regulation of food safety and quality has evolved over many years, although the three fundamental principles have always remained unscathed:

- the protection of the consumer by safeguarding health;
- the protection of the honest trader by preventing fraud and deception;
- the protection of freedom of choice and fair competition.

In 1266 the latter two fundamentals were protected by an Act concerned with the quantity of bread and ale supplied – the Assize of Bread and Ale, but the quality of food was for a long time left to subjective assessment. In the absence of scientific analysis of food, the adulteration of commodities was commonplace. Piecemeal legislation introduced to protect particular foods was ineffective. Eventually, in the mid-nineteenth century, chemical analysis of food was developed and using this as a means of providing evidence of adulteration, legislation was drafted as a general means of control. The Adulteration of Food Act 1860 was the first general enactment relating to the quality of all foods and was the forerunner of the Sale of Food and Drugs Act 1875, which contained much stronger provisions and which is recognised as the direct ancestor of today's food protection controls.

In the following years many areas of food were brought within the confines of legal control; ultimately these *ad hoc* statutes were consolidated by the Food and Drugs (Adulteration) Act 1928 and later by the Food and Drugs Act 1938. Minimum standards of composition and labelling were governed by the introduction of wartime legislation (Defence (Sale of Food) Regulations 1943). After several amending enactments, the Food and Drugs Act 1955 came into operation on 1 January 1956, along with its Scottish counterpart, the Food and Drugs (Scotland) Act 1956. This consolidated the 1938 Act and all the subsequent statutes so that legal controls of preparation, advertisements and sale of food for human consumption fell under a single Act.

Inevitably the 1955 and 1956 Acts became subject to later changes, such as the Local Government (Miscellaneous

Provisions) Act 1982 regulating the sale of food by hawkers and the Food and Drugs (Milk) Act 1970. These additions to the legal framework fragmented food control between a number of Acts of Parliament, and in 1984 it was again felt necessary to bring together all of the legal provisions relating to food control within England and Wales.

The Food Act 1984 was designed to consolidate provisions of the Food and Drugs Acts 1955 to 1982, the Sugar Act 1956, the Food and Drugs (Milk) Act 1970, s 7 (3) and (4) European Communities Act 1972, s 198 Local Government Act 1972, Part IX of the Local Government (Miscellaneous Provisions) Act 1982 and connected provisions. It came into force on 26 September 1984. Until the passing of the Food Safety Act 1990 it remained the principal statute controlling foodstuffs in England and Wales. However it provided little change to the old fundamental approach.

Food law advocates readily recognised this failure of the 1984 Act to impose satisfactory standards within the food industry and, it seems, so did the Government of that time, for in November 1983 it announced plans for a review of food legislation including the Scottish statutes. The Institution of Environmental Health Officers Congress in 1984 presented a policy paper which detailed the professional body's perceived view of the way forward. With this in mind the Government agreed that, although the existing legislation did, in its opinion, still provide some protection for the consumer the present laws were in need of revision. A consultative paper, *The Review Of Food Legislation*, was issued in December of that year and addressed several major issues. This document detailed the need to increase controls over the export of meat and other products, to strengthen the law regarding unfit food and to impose a stricter approach to the sale of novel foods and infant formulae. A rationalisation of the legislation applying to milk was planned, together with the introduction of a prior approval system for food premises and in-factory enforcement. Two other innovations were the adoption of due diligence defences where all reasonable precautions had been taken, and the use of codes of practice where regulations were not suitable. These two ideas were directly drawn from Robens' unique model, the Health and Safety at Work Act 1974, which has stood the test of time, embracing reasonably practicable defences and the concept of self regulation. (It also contained a general duty of care placed upon employers, but this notion has not been included in the food safety provisions.) Regulations and codes of practice specific in their subject matter supplemented the generalities of the principal Act and provided flexibility for new and changing situations.

In response to comments made by various interested parties during consultations, the Parliamentary Secretary initiated further discussions for the modernisation of the legislation.

Eventually July 1989 saw the production of the Government White Paper, *Food safety – protecting the consumer*, some five years after the consolidation of food law in 1984.

2. The Food Act 1984

In England and Wales the main governing principles pre-1990 were those in the 1984 Food Act – an enabling Act, with the general provisions being applicable to all foods and more specific requirements being imposed by detailed regulations. In order to understand the new controls it is necessary to give a short analysis of the content of the statute. Similar controls also existed within Scotland under the Food and Drugs (Scotland) Act 1956 and the amending enactments since that time. Scotland did not have, however, a consolidating statute such as the 1984 Food Act to bring all the various provisions under one enactment.

The 1984 Act was divided into seven parts covering the main points of law:

- Part I: Food generally;
- Part II: Milk dairies and cream substitutes;
- Part III: Markets;
- Part IV: Sale of food by hawkers;
- Part V: Sugar beet and cold storage;
- Part VI: Administration, enforcement and legal proceedings;
- Part VII: General and supplemental.

Provisions contained within the Act were of absolute liability, in that there was no general requirement to prove that an offence was committed intentionally or even knowingly. This was a common thread running through the Act. Four other common entities also existed:

(i) Throughout the provisions and any associated regulations "food" had a common interpretation: "to include drink, chewing gum and other products of a like nature and use, and articles and substances used as ingredients in the preparation of food and drink or of such products, but does not include water, live birds or fish or articles and substances used only as drugs" (s 131 Food Act 1984).

(ii) The legislation applied to food for human consumption. Any item commonly used for human consumption was presumed to be for such purpose if found on premises used for the preparation, storage or sale of that article. It was necessary for the defence to prove otherwise if this presumption was to be rebutted (s 98 Food Act 1984).

(iii) The legislation relating to composition and to labelling applied at every point at which food was sold.

(iv) Drafting of the legislation was purposely general, with detailed requirements being determined either by case law or by regulations.

Part I of the Act contained several provisions which formed the central theme of the legislation. Composition and labelling of food were directly controlled by restrictions on the preparation and sale of injurious foods together with the general protection of purchasers of food.

A person was guilty if he rendered food injurious to health by adding any substance to it, using any substance as an ingredient in its preparation, extracting any constituent or subjecting the food to any other process or treatment (s 1 Food Act 1984). The food had to be injurious to health and was not considered to be such merely because an ingredient in the food was injurious. For instance, in *Hull* v *Horsnell* (1904) the amount of injurious ingredient mixed was very small and the amount of food very large.

A person was guilty if he sold, to the purchaser's prejudice, any food intended for human consumption which was not of the nature, substance or quality demanded by the purchaser. The offences created (s 2 Food Act 1984) were the foundations of food law within the United Kingdom. Here the offence was simply to sell or for the intention to sell to exist, with no mention of the consumer's safety as such. Although a degree of overlap existed between the entities of nature, substance and quality (*Preston* v *Greenclose Ltd* (1975)), they were in fact three separate offences and the majority of case law is concerned with these points and with enforcement of this section.

"Not of the nature" applied principally to natural foods and was where the purchaser received something of a different variety or kind from what was requested – for example "Granny Smith" apples being sold as "Golden Delicious".

"Not of the substance" related to composition and covered adulteration offences and the presence of foreign bodies within foods, such as mould or glass in chocolate.

"Not of the quality" concerned the instance of a product not being up to the commercial quality expected by the ordinary buyer, for example where an ingredient may have been less than the amount required by regulation. However the presence of a foreign body in food has been held to make it also not of the quality demanded (*Newton* v *West Vale Creamery Co Ltd* (1956), a case which concerned a house fly in a milk bottle).

Whichever of the three options was chosen as the course of action, the sale had to be to the prejudice of the purchaser (*Smedleys Ltd* v *Breed* (1974)).

Quality or substance was used as an alternative to offences against s 1 where the focus was on the preparation and sale of injurious food (*Goulder* v *Rook* (1901)), and all three s 2 offences were appropriate as an alternative to s 6 (false or misleading descriptions of food as to its nature, substance or quality).

"Not of the substance" was an argument often relied upon when, although a foreign body or mould was present in the food, doubt existed as to whether this presence actually made the food unfit for human consumption – a necessary element for s 8 prosecutions (sale of unfit food). Other sections in Part I contained defences applicable to s 2 (s 3); ministerial powers to regulate the composition of particular foodstuffs (s 4); powers to require information from food manufacturers or importers regarding the ingredients included in any food-stuffs (s 5); and powers to regulate the manner in which food was described (s 7). The following additives, contaminants and compositional standards were covered by regulations:

Compositional standards

meat products
milk and milk products
poultry
natural mineral waters
soft drinks
bread
butter
cheese
cocoa and chocolate products
coffee and coffee products
condensed milk and dried milk
cream

curry powder
fish cakes
flour
fruit juices
honey
ice-cream
jams
liquid eggs
margarine
salad cream
suet
sugar products
tomato ketchup

Control of contaminants

chloroform
lead
arsenic
erucic acid

Control by process

irradiation

Control of additives

miscellaneous additives
stabilisers
emulsifiers
colours
antioxidants
mineral hydrocarbons
preservatives
solvents
sweeteners

Food unfit for human consumption was dealt with by s 8. This made it an offence for a person to sell, offer for sale or have in his possession for the purposes of sale or of preparation for sale any food intended for but unfit for, human consumption. Furthermore, any person who deposited with or consigned to another person any such unfit food for the purpose of sale, or of preparation for sale, was also guilty under this provision.

Whether the food was unfit was a question of fact in each case but from *David Greig Ltd* v *Goldfinch* (1961) it is clear that "unfit for human consumption" means more than just unsuitable.

The Act was an enabling instrument, with s 13 providing for ministerial regulations which governed food hygiene in various premises and laid down particular rules and requirements. Topics covered by subordinate legislation on food hygiene include:

- Food hygiene in premises;
- Food hygiene at market stalls and delivery vehicles;
- Food hygiene at docks etc;
- Imported food;
- Imported milk;
- Meat inspection;
- Meat sterilisation and staining;
- Milk-based products;
- Poultry meat hygiene;
- Shellfish;
- Slaughterhouse hygiene.

Under s 16 it was also a prerequisite for premises to meet the standards set by regulations before they could be registered for the sale or manufacture for sale or storage for sale of ice-cream, and for the preparation or manufacture of sausages or potted, pressed, pickled or preserved food intended for sale. It was an offence to carry out such activities from any premises not registered under this section.

Closure orders and emergency orders, formerly the provisions of the Food and Drugs (Control of Food Premises) Act 1976, were also available by virtue of ss 21 and 22. Section 21 provided that the local authority may apply to the court for a closure order in respect of food premises where a person had been convicted of an offence against regulations made under s 13. The offence included the carrying on of a food business at insanitary premises; and the court had to be satisfied that the premises would continue to be so used and that this would constitute a danger to health.

Notice of the intention to apply for this order must have been given to the defendant at least fourteen days before application. This, in effect, gave him a chance to rectify the situation. Where information was laid under s 21, the local authority could under s 22 apply to the court for an emergency closure order. The court had to be satisfied that the use of the premises involved imminent risk of danger to health, but even where this was shown to be so, it would not consider an application for such an order unless the person against whom information had been laid under s 21 had been given three clear days' notice in writing of the local authority's intention to apply for emergency closure. A serious deterrent to the use of these emergency closure powers was the availability of compensation claims. Where it was felt that the closure order had been granted by the court in respect of premises that were not in fact an imminent risk, then s 23 allowed interested persons to apply to the court for compensation. The court was then able to order the local authority to pay any amount the court thought proper in the circumstances. Compensation was due from the local authority because it was its information which had initially indicated the presence of an imminent risk.

Compensation could only be claimed from the local authority if loss had directly occurred as a result of the order, but this was almost certainly to be the case within the food industry.

Part II of the Act controlled milk, dairies and cream substitutes, covering the introduction of specific regulations for hygiene within dairies, adulteration of milk, registration of dealers and the special designations of milk and their uses.

Markets (Part III), sale of food by hawkers (Part IV) and sugar beet and cold storage (Part V) were also covered by the Act.

Powers of sampling and analysis, enforcement and legal proceedings were detailed within Part VI. The power to enter premises (s 87) allowed an authorised officer to enter any premises at a reasonable hour provided that he produced, if required, a duly authenticated document showing his authority. The purpose of entry had to be to ascertain if there was any contravention of the Act or of any regulations made under it, or to enable the council to perform its duties under the Act. A warrant to enter, issued by a justice of the peace, was available in certain circumstances and it was an absolute offence under s 91 to obstruct wilfully any officer acting in the execution of his duties under the Act.

Despite the detailed controls contained within the 1984 Act, the fact remained that this piece of legislation was a consolidating statute which served only to reiterate age-old principles under one statutory umbrella. Consumers needed to be reassured about the food available on the market, but this assurance was sometimes difficult to come by due to the problems of enforcement. Premises which were a risk to public health could trade for up to three days while legalities were completed for their closure; there was no satisfactory control over the temperature at which food was stored, and compensation rights of defendants inevitably caused too much caution by public agencies who were financially accountable to the electorate – a local authority could be liable to pay large amounts of compensation in respect of the emergency closure of food businesses or in respect of the deterioration of goods which had been detained for sampling pending the outcome of analysis.

These concerns and many others prompted the production of the White Paper in 1989 which attempted to resolve some of the underlying problems.

3. Effect of European Economic Community legislation

Any consideration of United Kingdom legislation must include the effect that Europe, and in particular the formation of a single European market, has on food law in Britain. Britain's position as a member state of the European Economic Community had a significant impact on the production of the White Paper, with national legislation being introduced or amended at an alarming rate due to the intervention and growing involvement of Brussels. Since United Kingdom accession to the European Communities in 1973, Community initiatives have become a major part of the British legal system. Several pieces of subordinate legislation have arisen from attempts to harmonise food standards across Europe. Implementation of Community policy requires the establishment of specific provisions within our own legal framework.

The European objective is the creation of a single "common market" with no restrictions on trade between member states. For this to exist, there is a definite need for a set of common controls, with the broad principles being contained within the Treaty of Rome 1957 (together with its subsequent amendments). The detailed requirements take the form of regulations and directives.

Article 30 of the Treaty provides that "[Q]uantitative restrictions on imports ... shall ... be prohibited between member states". This provision by virtue of Article 36 has a number of exceptions, one of which concerns the passage of foodstuffs and the protection of humans, animals or plants. Essentially this exception means that within the European Economic Community the only restriction on the free passage of legally produced foodstuffs from one member state to another will be where there is an obvious threat to public health. In every other way, British food legislation must be in harmony with the policies of the European Commission by 31 December 1992.

Since the case commonly known as *Cassis de Dijon* (1979), barriers to trade are likely to be removed by way of judicial decisions which permit any product legally sold in one member state to be legally sold in another, a principle established by the European Court. Briefly the case concerned a blackcurrant liqueur, Cassis, manufactured in France. When German importers tried to sell it in Germany they found that, according to German law, it did not have the required amount of alcohol in it. The importers appealed to the European Court against a decision to prevent them from selling Cassis, and obtained a judgment against Germany based upon the premise that German law was a non-tariff barrier to trade. The irony of such a judgment is that importers can legally sell Cassis throughout the Community, but a German producer could not sell a product with a similar alcohol content made in his own country because he remains subject to German law.

Despite the intervention of case law which serves to assist harmonisation, some method of incorporating Community changes into our own legal framework still has to be provided. Directives already in force in 1973 were included in the treaty of accession, but new provisions on food had to be implemented as and when they arose. The basic food legislation existing at that time (the Food and Drugs Act 1955) was therefore chosen as a means of securing harmonisation with any new European initiatives. These means were reiterated within s 119 (1) Food Act 1984 which provided ministers with the power to issue national regulations which would ensure the administration, execution and enforcement of directly applicable Community provisions relating to food. The phrase "directly applicable Community provisions" related here to European Economic Community regulations and enabled them to be enforced as if they had been made under the 1984 Act. It was necessary under s 119 to be aware of the distinction between EC regulations and directives: while subs (1) dealt with the former, subs (2) talked of Community obligations or "directives". The methods of implementing directives were by way of ss 4, 7 and 97 supplemented by s 119(2).

Ministers were empowered by s 4 to make national regulations in the interests of public health, or otherwise for the protection of the public, and also where they are called for by Community obligations. Section 7 provided for regulations to be made which imposed requirements and regulated the labelling, marketing, advertising or description of food intended for sale for human consumption. This section extended the regulation-making process for labelling and other requirements to include instances where Community obligations called for such controls. By s 97, regulations under s 4 or s 7 could prescribe analysis for the purpose of ascertaining the presence or absence of a specified substance. Furthermore, in any relevant proceedings this prescribed method was deemed to be preferred evidence. Thus where regulations made under s 4 or s 7 were in pursuance of Community obligations, by s 97 they could also include Community methods of analysis which for all practical purposes were the only methods of analysis which could be used.

The supplemental provision of s 119(2) allowed the minister to make further national regulations in addition to those above so as to comply with any Community obligation (directive) or provision. These national regulations covered the subject matter of food sampling methods dealing with food samples and the methods of analysing, testing or examining food samples. Section 119 also stated that any regulations made under subs (2) could modify or exclude any of the provisions of the Food Act 1984 relating to sampling, analysis or any of the other parameters mentioned above.

This produced an exact method by which member state legislation could be brought into line with European

Community requirements without removing completely the legislative power of Britain.

It is essential that any new food legislation should incorporate a similar enabling measure, especially in view of the European Community Directive "the Official Control of Foodstuffs" (89/397/EEC), and the promise of the long-awaited food hygiene directive. A more simplified way of integrating Community requirements is necessary although it is important to retain the non-statute making element of the enabling provision. This will ensure constant revision of legislation in the light of developments on a European scale.

4. Food safety – protecting the consumer

The White Paper, *Food safety – protecting the consumer* (July 1989), set out the principles of food hygiene and food safety which the Government had decided would provide increased protection for the consumer. It outlined the proposals for a completely new piece of legislation that would reorganise the current statutory framework to meet with tomorrow's needs. It envisaged one enactment applicable throughout the whole of England, Wales and Scotland.

In the foreword to the White Paper the Minister of Agriculture, Fisheries and Food stated that "protecting the consumer remains the Government's overriding concern". There was little doubt that anyone disagreed with the importance of this protection; indeed, many critics felt that the proposals did not go far enough and that considerable amendment to the content would be necessary to achieve any truly protective standard. Nevertheless, the food safety strategy described in the White Paper stated that the Government:

● should insist on stringent hygiene standards throughout the food chain;

● controlled the use of additives such as colourings and preservatives;

● monitored chemical contaminants and laid down stringent limits, often with very wide margins of safety;

- aimed to ensure that the danger to health from microbiological contamination is kept to an absolute minimum;
- assessed novel foods and processes to ensure their safety.

In addition it was felt that any legal framework should:

- set controls and standards on the basis of independent scientific advice;
- protect consumers from fraudulent and misleading claims about the nature, content and safety of food;
- require clear information to be provided on the content and composition of food.

Within this strategy the Government indicated that it was determined to ensure the widest availability of wholesome attractive foods throughout the country, but whilst encouraging this freedom of choice, it was also committed to giving the highest priority to the safety of the consumer.

Furthermore, against a background of ever greater consumer choice and technological changes within the food industry, the Government indicated that it was dedicated to anticipating future needs by developing the existing law in such a way as to increase the ability to take swift and effective action.

But of the sixty-eight pages within the White Paper, only eight actually dealt with the evident problems of food law. These few pages were the hopes for food safety in the future. A major aim of the new legislative requirements and radical reforms was to ensure that modern food technology and distribution methods were safe and that food was not misleadingly labelled or presented. The Government was in favour of reinforcement of the existing powers and penalties against law breakers. Administratively, the two main objectives were first to ensure that new EC directives on food could be implemented and, secondly, to streamline the legislation by combining the Acts applicable to England and Wales and to Scotland.

To fulfil these aims the White Paper included seven major proposals for the new legislation: maintenance of food hygiene;protection of the consumer against injurious food;

protection of the consumer against food that is not of the nature, substance or quality demanded by the purchaser; protection of the consumer against unfit food; protection of the consumer against false or misleading labelling; introduction of powers to make regulations on the composition and labelling of food, and the regulatory control of the hygiene of food.

These seven major proposals formed the basis of the new legislative intent. The first concerned tighter controls on unfit food and food not of the nature, substance or quality demanded. Here certain enforcement powers were to be given by the Act in relation to possession for sale, as well as sale itself. Thus the powers could be exercised before the goods were put on sale. Under the White Paper, food suspected of being unfit would be detainable by enforcement officers pending the outcome of investigations.

It was envisaged that new enforcement measures would be introduced to strengthen the existing system. This could be achieved by extending enforcement in food processing factories, for example. Environmental health officers already have the power to inspect such places in relation to hygiene, and the Health and Safety Executive has corresponding powers for matters relating to health and safety. The new proposals would extend this so that trading standards officers can inspect the processing unit for compositional and labelling matters. It has been argued that this should be taken even one stage further to include inspections by qualified process technicians who would concern themselves with the technological aspects such as the process fault, not evident from a hygiene inspection, that caused the botulism problem in hazelnut yoghurt. Enforcement officers would also be able to apply for whole batches of food to be condemned.

Another main proposal was provision for the registration of food premises which would assist the enforcement agencies by enabling them to identify premises more readily. Some premises had to be registered already under the old legislation (under s 16 Food Act 1984 where ice-cream is stored or sold etc); but, to be really effective, the definition of food premises would have to cover all types of food business not traditionally associated with premises. Indeed, registration is no guarantee of safe procedures and practice, and a licensing system would give local authorities much more control over standards.

Coupled with the idea of registration in the White Paper was the notion of speeding up the closure procedures for premises which do not comply with the necessary requirements. The ability to serve notices on premises where problems have to be rectified would speed up the legal process. For any real improvement the process would also have to be simplified.

Enhanced powers to control contaminants and residues, such as antibiotic or veterinary drug residues in meat, were advocated. These powers would extend to residues that might arise from bad practices either on the farm or in the processing of foods. Emergency control orders would be introduced so that where it was necessary to recall dangerous foods or to prevent the importation of adulterated goods (such as the contaminated wine problem in 1989), stock could be confiscated and imports stopped. This would be a useful power over and above mere reliance upon the co-operation of manufacturers and traders, which had always been a corner-stone of the system. Training was detailed as a general aid to improving hygiene conditions through education and self regulation. The White Paper talked of a provision for the training of food handlers in industry with regulations laying down the nature of training to be given in food hygiene. The food industry, the Institution of Environmental Health Officers and other bodies already run courses designed to fulfil these objectives, and the intention would be to build on existing good practice so that more persons take up the initiative.

The White Paper proposed changes in legal defences available to defendants who are charged with an offence under the food laws. Currently, other consumer legislation makes it an offence for a trader to sell consumer goods unless he has taken all reasonable precautions to ensure that the goods are safe (Consumer Protection Act 1987).

This is not so with food law, and retailers could rely upon the statutory warranty defence which allowed an easy escape under the claim that all they did was to sell food manufactured by some other person. A more accountable approach is the intended "due diligence" defence, where certain circumstances are detailed in the legislation whereby a retailer or other buyer would be deemed to have shown due diligence in the transaction. If he had not shown such care, the due diligence defence would not be available to him in any proceedings instigated. The specification of certain circumstances will reduce the uncertainty as to what due diligence actually entails. In essence the new defence will mean that to avoid liability for defective foods, traders will have to take more care about what they buy and how they treat it once it is in their possession.

In addition to these proposals, the Government also indicated that it would ensure extended powers to adapt the law to technological developments such as genetic manipulation and food irradiation. It included a control framework for such foods, with centralised licensing of irradiation facilities, detailed inspection and supervision by specialists and informative labelling of irradiated goods so that consumers know what they are buying.

In its brief conclusion, the White Paper stated that the proposals for new legislation reflected the Government's continuing commitment to the highest possible standards of food safety and consumer protection, now and in the future. November 1989 saw the production of the Food Safety Bill and many of the proposals contained within the earlier White Paper were included. The true suitability and practicality of the new framework was put to the test as the Bill underwent its passage through Parliament.

The Food Safety Bill completed its committee stage on 3 April 1990 following five sittings of the committee with three divisions. In all, 175 amendments and 7 new clauses were considered; of these only 35 amendments were accepted. Following the report stage, it was clear that one important change had taken place concerning water, a commodity used in every single food business. After representations from Mr M Taylor, Mr J Boswell and Mr C Gill, the Parliamentary Secretary to the Ministry of Agriculture, Fisheries and Food (MAFF) proposed an amendment to clarify the definition of drink to ensure that all water from the point of supply was included in the scope of the Bill. The amendment was accepted and this effectively brought tap water under the statutory umbrella. Other significant proposals were lost, including those concerning the creation of a single independent food safety agency and of a general duty on operators of food businesses to ensure the fitness of food and the health and safety of the consumer, together with proposals for the extension of time allowed for the analysis of foodstuffs, and for further restrictions on irradiation. This undoubtedly provoked the cynicism with which consumer groups viewed the MAFF assurances that the new provisions "provide a tough new framework for food safety legislation", a statement made just after the Act received the Royal Assent on 29 June 1990.

The main provisions of the Food Safety Act include:

- a strengthening of the powers of enforcement including detention and seizure of food and in-factory enforcement;
- an umbrella offence of supplying food that fails to comply with food safety requirements;
- powers to require the registration of food premises, allow the issue of improvement notices and swift closure of premises if public health is threatened;
- adaptation of the law to take account of technological developments;
- powers for Ministers to tackle potentially serious problems with emergency closure orders;
- stronger controls over contaminants and residues;
- modernisation of the system of statutory defences to cover all of those involved in the supply of food;
- tougher penalties.

All of these provisions are applicable throughout the whole of England, Scotland and Wales.

Chapter 2

Commencement and related provisions

The first part of this chapter explains the way in which the Government has chosen to bring the Act into force; the middle sections provide an insight into the effect of the Act upon subordinate legislation already in operation before its commencement and its amendment of other statutory provisions; in the final section the various terms and definitions used within the Act are summarised.

1. Commencement

On 29 June 1990, the Food Safety Act received royal assent. It was intended to make new provisions to replace the Food Act 1984 and the Food and Drugs (Scotland) Act 1956, and to amend Parts III and V of the Food Act 1984, and Part I of the Food and Environment Protection Act 1985. It provides one enabling statute for the control of food safety within England, Scotland and Wales. Northern Ireland will be subject to its own, but similar, enactment (s 60(5)).

Of immediate effect under s 60 were emergency control orders and amendments to the Food and Environment Protection Act 1985 and the Food Act 1984.

Section 13 makes emergency control orders, initiated by the Minister, immediately available as a means of controlling commercial operations involving food, food source materials or contact materials which may involve imminent risk of

19

injury to health. The Minister may make an order prohibiting the carrying out of any such operations.

The other immediate provisions concerned amendments to existing legislation. Therefore, from 29 June 1990 s 51 of the Act amended s 1 Food and Environment Protection Act 1985 (FEPA 1985). From that date s 1 includes the power to make emergency control orders. Under s 1 FEPA 1985, any escape of substances which were likely to create a hazard to human health by human consumption could be controlled by an order made by the Minister. Statutory instrument required the quantity of the material which had escaped and the circumstances relating to it to be taken into account when determining the hazard. The order contained provisions designating the area to be controlled together with details of emergency provisions required to deal with the escape.

The amendments to this section by the Act concern the replacement of "escape" by "circumstances", a much wider approach. Where food becomes unsuitable for human consumption due to "circumstances", it remains possible to control the situation by order as before, but many more situations will now be caught by the use of the word "circumstances". The section can now be used to deal with any incident likely to create a hazard to human health by the human consumption of food. "Designated circumstances" are substituted in s 1 for the phrase "a designated incident" and are given the definition of "circumstances or suspected circumstances to which an emergency order refers in pursuance of s 1(5)."

On 2 July 1990 Commencement No 1 Order (1990 No 1383) was made bringing into effect on the following day provisions which were needed to give full effect to s 13 (emergency control orders) and s 51 (amendment to FEPA 1985). For the purpose of control orders, the definition of food, the extended meaning of sale, presumptions as to food, certain enforcement and administrative provisions, defences, the general interpretation section and the application of the Act to the Scilly Isles, Channel Islands and territorial waters, were brought into force. For the purpose of amending FEPA 1985, the definition of food, general interpretation and details of other amendments in s 3 were given effect, but only for use in connection with ss 13 and 51. For any other purposes they were not given legal force.

Paragraphs 12–15 of Sch 2 to the Act amend Part V (sugar beet and cold storage) of the Food Act 1984. Section 52 gives effect to those amendments immediately. The old definition of "Company" (British Sugar Company plc) in s 68 (1) and (2) Food Act 1984 is replaced by the wider and more appropriate "processors of home grown beet". Orders for ensuring that programmes are effected for research and education into the growing of home grown beet now have to be made by statutory instrument. A new s 69(A) is inserted which allows the Minister to serve notice compelling a processor to give information to the Minister where determination of crop price is to be made under s 69(1) Food Act 1984.

This area of food legislation is derived from ss 18 and 35 Sugar Act 1956, and was originally included in the Food Act 1984 because of the relationship between ministerial powers in respect of sugar beet and the powers of local authorities in respect of cold storage facilities at markets (s 70 Food Act 1984).

Paragraph 16 of Sch 2, which provides that the above-mentioned s 70 Food Act 1984 (provision of cold storage) shall cease to have effect, was not brought into immediate operation with the other provisions mentioned above, and this is unlikely to change until 1 January 1991. All other main provisions within the Act are likely to take effect on this date, provided that this becomes the day "the Ministers may by order appoint" (s 60(3)). Section 60 also allows this order to include transitional adaptations of any provisions in force before the date of the order, or of any provisions brought into force by it. These adaptations also apply to provisions repealed by the Act, but which are not repealed at the date of the order or are not repealed by that order, keeping the provisions in force until their repeal becomes effective.

Most of the associated regulations, orders and codes of practice, which will provide the detailed control, will be brought into force in batches in January, April and July 1991 by the laying of statutory instruments. The effectiveness of this new legal framework will depend very much on the willingness of Government to provide strong subordinate legislative initiatives. Full consultation with all interested parties will occur before any statutory instrument or code of practice is given effect. Their introduction will be a continual process, allowing easy adaptation of the law to suit new developments. The extension of food law to Crown premises is unlikely to take place before 1992, despite recent findings that National Health Service premises are benefiting from the exposure to legal food hygiene controls.

2. Transitional provisions, savings and repeals

Schedule 3 to the Act lists those enactments which have been slightly amended by the new statute, but which remain in effect by virtue of s 59 and are unaltered in their content. These enactments are:

1936 The Public Health Act

1963 The London Government Act

1967 The Farm and Garden Chemicals Act

     The Agriculture Act

1968 The Trades Description Act

     The Medicines Act (inclusion of facilities for microbiology examination of drugs provision)

     The Transport Act

1971 The Tribunals and Inquiries Act

1972 The Agriculture (Miscellaneous Provisions) Act

     The Poisons Act

     The Local Government Act

1974 The Slaughterhouses Act

1976 The Licensing (Scotland) Act

     The Weights and Measures Act

1979 The Hydrocarbons Oil Duties Act

1980 The Slaughter of Animals (Scotland) Act

1982 The Civic Government (Scotland) Act

1984 The Public Health (Control of Disease) Act (insertion of s 28 Food Act 1984 as s 20(1)(A) which lists the diseases that require persons to stop work to prevent the spread of disease)

1985 The Food and Environment Protection Act

     The Local Government Act

     The Weights and Measures Act

1986 The Agriculture Act

1986   The National Health Service (Amendment) Act
1987   The Consumer Protection Act
1988   The Road Traffic Offenders Act

Section 59 (2) enables the modification of local Acts and subordinate legislation not covered in s 3, to bring them into line with the new legislation. Two sets of conflicting legislation cannot exist and therefore this subsection allows for a remedy should such a disparity arise.

As well as implementing minor amendments to principal Acts, s 59(3) allows for the retention of any regulations and orders made under the Food Act 1984, the Food and Drugs (Scotland) Act 1956, or the Importation of Milk Act 1983 which were in force at the time the Act took effect. These regulations are listed in s 4 together with any amendments and have effect as if made under the relevant provisions of the Act. They therefore fall within the category of "regulations made under the Act", a phrase used throughout the statute.

Transitional savings also apply to disqualification of caterers orders (s 14 Food Act 1984), food hygiene by-laws (s 15 Food Act 1984) and closure orders (s 21 Food Act 1985; s1 Control of Food Premises (Scotland) Act 1977). Any orders made under s 14 in relation to the disqualification of persons, or under ss 1 and 21 for the closure of food premises, remain in force until the time stated in the order expires, provided that the orders were made before s 5 of the Act came into force. Section 5 repeals those provisions relating to orders and by-laws; once the repealing measures of this section pass their operative date, the powers under ss 1, 14 and 21 cease to have effect and any orders made after that time are invalid.

Any by-laws made under s 15 Food Act 1984 before the commencement of s 5 will remain intact only in so far as they complement or reiterate any regulations made under the Act or any regulations saved by s 3. If a conflict does arise between valid by-laws and any regulatory provision, the regulations shall prevail. To determine whether by-laws are valid, thought must be given to whether:

(a)   they were made before the commencement of s 5 Food Safety Act 1990;

(b)   they are *intra vires*;

(c) ss 235–238 of the Local Government Act 1972 (procedure for making by-laws) has been complied with; and

(d) they are consistent with general law.

On this last point alone, any by-laws conflicting with regulations made under the Act would be seen as invalid.

Schedule 5 contains the repeals effected by the Act, and it is important to note here that, of the Food Act 1984, Part III (markets), Part V (sugar beet and cold storage) (as amended), and some of Parts VI and VII remain good law. However, the whole of the Food and Drugs (Scotland) Act is repealed.

3. Amendments

Paragraphs 1–11 of Sch 2 amend Part III of the Food Act 1984 which relates to markets. The establishment or acquisition of markets under s 50(3) Food Act 1984 is simplified in its wording. This section repeated the provisions of the Food and Drugs Act 1955 as amended by the Local Government Act 1972, providing for the establishment or acquisition of markets at the discretion of the district council. It is important to remember that these provisions, as amended by the Local Government Act 1972, extend to all London boroughs (s 54 and Sch 13 London Government Act 1963 as amended by s 134 and Sch 10 Food Act 1984). Furthermore, of the two kinds of markets that exist, statutory and franchise (set up by charter and letters patent of the Crown), s 50 deals only with the former.

Injunctions for disturbance of markets will continue to be available. The wrong of disturbance of a market has always existed at common law, and therefore an interlocutory injunction can be granted restraining a licence to hold a market once disturbance had been shown. Difficulties with injunctions may arise if there is, however, no apparent threat of repetition (*Birmingham Corporation* v *Foster* (1894); *Hailsham Cattle Market Co* v *Tolman* (1915)).

The power to charge for the weighing of cattle, sheep or swine at a market is extended to the charging for provision of cold stores or refrigeration used for meat and other articles of food by the insertion of a new subs (2) to s 53 Food Act 1984. With respect to charges, the level set will depend upon the success in profit terms of the market. Whitford J, in *Ricketts* v *Havering London Borough Council* (1980), stated that "a market authority has a discretion to impose reasonable charges and it is reasonable to take the view that the market profits should contribute to the general rates fund". Section 70 Food Act 1984 (cold storage) is repealed and replaced by a similar provision, through insertion of a new s 57A. The use of a new term "market authority" is evident. However, the need of a market authority to obtain consent from a local authority in whose area it intends to provide cold storage continues to be necessary. Such consent cannot be unreasonably withheld (s 57A(3)), with "unreasonable" being a matter determined by the Ministers on referral to them. In cases of referral, the provisions of the Local Government Act 1972 (s 250(1) – (5)) relating to local inquiries apply.

Paragraph 10 of Sch 2 increases the power of a local authority which maintains a market to make by-laws; such a local authority is now classed as the market authority by virtue of a new definition provided by the Act. Under s 60 Food Act 1984, by-laws could be made for regulating the use of the market place, for preventing nuisances or obstructions and for regulating porters and carriers resorting to the market.

Schedule 2 para 10 Food Safety Act 1990 now includes the power to make by-laws for preventing the spread of fires in the market, provided that the local fire authority has been consulted beforehand. "Fire authority" is given the meaning of an authority exercising the functions of a fire authority under the Fire Services Act 1947. This is an important inclusion and confirms general awareness of the need for the prevention of fires and preparation for emergencies. Any by-laws made under these provisions may be confirmed by the Secretary of State upon application by the local authority (s 121 Food Act 1984), but confirmation will never validate an improper by-law. Again, by-laws which are unreasonable or in general restraint of trade are *ultra vires*; with respect to markets, however, by-laws can contain a prohibition of some sales in particular sale rings provided that the sale is not to be by public auction (*Strike* v *Collins* (1886)).

"Market authority" is given a slightly wider definition in that it does not now apply only to local authorities which establish or acquire a market under the provisions of s 50 Food Act 1984. Instead, it refers to a local authority which maintains a market which has been so established or acquired. Before the Act, the market authority had to be the local authority establishing or acquiring the market. Now the essence is simply on maintenance and it matters not which authority establishes or acquires, so long as these acts were done legally under s 50(1) Food Act 1984 or an earlier enactment.

4. Definitions

Throughout the Act are a number of key terms and definitions which are constantly used and referred to. Within s 53(1)(a) a general interpretation is given for the majority of these. Other sections, as listed in subs (2), also contain various definitions of phrases and terms which are necessary for the interpretation of some provisions.

In addition to these literal explanations, common law has, in some instances, added to the general application of particular terms. Below is a summary of the main definitions, some of which have been further expanded in Chapter 3. The section where the definition is found within the Act is given first followed by the Act's interpretation. Any important common law applications are then briefly discussed.

Advertisement (s 53(1)): includes any notice, circular, label, wrapper, invoice or other document, and any public announcement made orally or by the transmission or production of light or sound. Advertise is defined in these terms also.

Analysis (s 53(1)): includes microbiological assay and any technique for establishing the composition of food. Analyse is defined in these terms also. Although microbiological assay is included expressly, the literal meaning of analysis does not include other forms of biological assay. Therefore, milk tests such as the phosphatase, the methylene blue, the resazurin, the plate count, the microscopic count and the coliform bacillus test, which fall within the category of biological assay, are not for the purposes of the Act classed as analysis.

Other examinations which are not "analysis" include organoleptic examination such as those of natural foods, fish, fruit and the like which is carried out to determine their nature or variety, and the alpha-amylase test prescribed for liquid egg.

Animal (s 53(1)): includes any creature other than a bird or fish.

Article (s 53(1)): is not a live animal or bird. Neither is it a live fish which is not used for human consumption while it is alive. Gas and water are articles (*Ferens* v *O'Brien* (1883)), but electricity is not (*Granada TV Network Ltd* v *Kerridge* (1963)). Other than these specifically mentioned entities, common law has established that "article" has many different meanings and must be looked at in context.

Authorised officer of a food authority (s 5(6)): any person authorised in writing, by a food authority, to act under the provisions of the Act. This person does not have to be an officer of the authority provided that he is correctly authorised, and the authorisation can be in either general or specific terms. However, the Ministers may provide by regulations that a person has to have explicit qualifications before he can be so authorised.

Business (s 1(3)): includes the undertaking of canteen, club, school, hospital or institution, whether carried on for profit or not, and any profit-making undertaking or activity carried on by a public or local authority.

Other undertakings not mentioned above have to fall within the literal meaning of business in that they have to be run for profit. If they are not carried on for gain, they do not constitute a business.

Commercial operation (s 1(3)): when using the terms "food or contact material", commercial operation is defined as:

(a) selling, possessing for sale and offering, exposing or advertising for sale;

(b) consigning, delivering or serving by way of sale;

(c) preparing for sale in the case of food, and in the case of any contact material manufacturing or producing for the purpose of sale;

(d) presenting, labelling or wrapping for the purpose of sale;

(e) storing or transporting for the purpose of sale;

(f) importing and exporting.

Commercial operation in relation to food source means deriving food from the source for the purpose of sale or purposes connected with sale.

Contact material (s 1(3)): any article or substance intended to come into contact with food.

Container (s 53(1)): includes baskets, pails, trays, packages or receptacles of any kind. They may be open or closed.

Contravention (s 53(1)): failure to comply with a legal requirement of the Act, or failure to comply with the legal requirement of any regulations or orders made under the Act. This includes any regulations and orders retained by s 59(3) which have effect as if made under the relevant provisions of the Act.

Cream (s 53(1)): the separated part of milk which is rich in fat and which has been separated by skimming or some other means.

Emergency control order (s 13(1)): an order prohibiting the carrying out of commercial operations which involve food, food sources or contact materials of any class or description, where the operations involve or may involve imminent risk of injury to health.

Emergency prohibition notices (s 12(1)): a notice served on the proprietor of a business where the health risk condition has been fulfilled in relation to any food business. In certain cases this notice will prohibit the use of a process, treatment, premises or equipment for the purposes of a food business and this prohibition is known as the appropriate prohibition.

Emergency prohibition order (s 12(2)): an order made by a magistrates' court in England or by a sheriff in Scotland, imposing the appropriate prohibition with respect to any food business. The authorised officer must apply to the court or the sheriff for the order, satisfying them that the health risk condition is fulfilled with respect to the food business. Failure to comply with a court order carries appropriate penalties and is classed as contempt of court.

Enforcement authority (s 6(1)): the authority which enforces and executes the provisions of the Act or any regulations or orders made under it. The actual authority will depend upon which authority is given enforcement powers by the Minister. Whichever is empowered for particular provisions will be the enforcement authority for those provisions.

Equipment (s 53(1)): includes any apparatus.

Examination (s 28(2)): means microbiological examination. "Examine" is to be defined in these terms.

Exportation and importation (s 53(1)): means the same as under the Customs and Excise Management Act 1979. Export and import are to be defined accordingly in those terms also. Under s 5 of the 1979 Act importation of goods is deemed to be:

● when a ship carrying goods by sea comes within the limits of a port;

● when an aircraft carrying goods lands within the United Kingdom or goods are unloaded from an aircraft into the United Kingdom, whichever is the sooner;

● where goods brought in by land cross the border into Northern Ireland.

Exportation is where the ship leaves the port limits, an aircraft takes off and where goods cross the border out of Northern Ireland.

Fish (s 53(1)): includes crustaceans and molluscs.

Food (s 1(1),(2) and (4)): includes drink, chewing gum and products of a like nature and use, articles and substances of no nutritional value or those used as ingredients in the preparation of food (as expressed by s 1) which are used for human consumption. It does not include live animals, birds and some live fish, or fodder or feeding stuff for them. Neither does it include controlled drugs and certain medicinal products. Water is now included as food, but only from the point of supply in food production premises. At common law, food has been taken to include products mistakenly served for food (*Meah* v *Roberts; Lansley* v *Roberts* (1978)).

Food authority (s 5): for England and Wales, the borough, district or county council of each London borough, district or non-metropolitan county, the common council of the City of London (including the Temples) and the appropriate treasurer for the Inner or Middle Temples are to be classed as the food authorities.

For Scotland the food authorities are the islands or district councils.

Where orders made under other legislation assign particular functions to a port health authority (ss 2 and 7 Public Health (Control of Disease) Act 1984 or s 172 Public Health (Scotland) Act 1987), to a joint board for a united district (s 6 Public Health Act 1936), or to a single authority for a metropolitan county (Sch 8 Local Government Act 1985), these authorities are classed as the food authority for these functions.

The Minister can by order provide that any particular function or functions be exercised solely by any one of these authorities.

Food business (s 1(3)): those businesses where commercial operations in respect of food or food sources are carried out. The use of the word "business" indicates that the commercial operations must be carried on for profit unless they fall within undertakings classed as canteens, clubs, schools, hospitals or institutions – such undertakings are classed as a business whether run for profit or not.

Food premises (s 1(3)): premises used for the purpose of a food business. Again the terms "business" and "food business" must be satisfied. "Premises" is given a definition in its own right within subs (3); provided that this is also satisfied, the term "food premises" will attach to the particular building or part of it.

Food safety requirements and related expressions (s 8(2)): these requirements can be defined thus, that food has not been rendered injurious to health, that it is not unfit for human consumption and that it is not contaminated to the extent that its use for human consumption would be considered unreasonable. "Rendered injurious to health" is given meaning by reference to s 7 of the Act, which lists those operations which can cause food to become injurious. Contamination can be by extraneous matter or otherwise, and "unfit" means more than just unsuitable but not necessarily injurious or dangerous.

Food source (s 1(3)): is any growing crop of live animal, bird or fish from which food is intended to be derived. The way in which food may be derived is by harvest, slaughter, milking, collection of eggs or otherwise. This essentially covers any process by which food is obtained.

Functions (s 53(1)): includes powers and duties.

Human consumption (s 53(1)): includes use in the preparation of food for human consumption.

Improvement notice (s 10(1)): a notice served on the proprietor of a food business where an authorised officer of an enforcement authority has reasonable grounds to believe that the proprietor is not complying with particular regulations. These regulations fall into two categories: those made for controlling the preparation of food, and those made for securing the observance of hygienic conditions and practices within commercial food operations.

This notice has to state the reasonable grounds of the officer for believing non-compliance, the matters which constitute non-compliance, remedial measures to secure compliance and a time limit in excess of fourteen clear days within which a remedy must be effected.

Its form and service must be in accordance with the methods laid down by the Act under the authentication and service of documents.

Injury to health and injurious to health (s 7(3)): injury includes any permanent or temporary impairment, and injurious to health is to be thought of in the same terms.

To constitute an offence it must be found as a fact that the end product is rendered injurious to health (*Hull* v *Horsnell* (1904)), and it must be injurious to a substantial portion of the community likely to use the product (*Cullen* v *McNair* (1908)).

Knacker's yard (s 53(1)): means any premises used in connection with the business of slaughtering, flaying or cutting up of animals where the flesh of those animals is not intended for human consumption. To constitute a knacker's yard, its use should be regular and not on the odd occasion only. Where there is only an occasional use, the premises would be outside the definition (*Perrins* v *Smith* (1946)).

Milk (s 53(1)): includes cream and skimmed or separated milk, but does not appear to include dried or condensed milk for the purposes of the Act.

31

Milk must be as it comes from the animal, and must be unadulterated. Note that failing to maintain even distribution of fat throughout the cream can be held to be adulteration (*Duke* v *Gower* (1892)).

Minister (the) (s 4(1) and (2)): in England and Wales this is the Minister of Agriculture, Fisheries and Food or the Secretary of State. In Scotland it is the Secretary of State.

Ministers (the) (s 4(1)): in England they are the Minister of Agriculture, Fisheries and Food, and the Secretaries of State concerned with health acting jointly. In Wales they are the Minister of Agriculture, Fisheries and Food, and the Secretaries of State for food and health acting jointly.

In Scotland it is the Secretary of State.

Occupier (s 53(1)): means the master, commander or other person in charge of any ship or aircraft specified in an order made under s 1 (3), and of any vehicle, stall or other place. At common law *Robinson* v *Bridge* (1870) held that the occupier is the person having physical control or possession of the premises.

Officer (s 53(1)): includes servant.

Premises (s 1(3)): includes place, vehicle, stall or movable structure and any ship or aircraft specified and described in an order made by the Minister.

Where circumstances dictate it, common law will not extend the meaning of premises in s 1 beyond its ordinary and natural definition, which is taken to be land or buildings on land. However, this remains unimportant to the Act provided that the structure is a place, vehicle, stall or movable structure. Should it be incapable of being classed as one of these, the circumstances surrounding the situation will determine whether "premises" can be applied.

Note, however, that until April 1992 Crown premises are exempted from the provisions of the Act.

Preparation (s 53(1)): in relation to food includes manufacture and any form of processing or treatment. "Preparation for sale" includes packaging, and "prepare for sale" is to be thought of in these terms also.

Presentation of food (s 53(1)): includes the shape, appearance, packaging and arrangement during exposure for sale of food. It also includes the setting in which food is displayed with a view to sale, but does not include labelling or advertising of food. "Presentation" is also to be thought of in these terms.

Prohibition order (s 11(5)): an order made by the court which imposes the appropriate prohibition on the proprietor of a food business. The proprietor must have been convicted of an offence under regulations made for controlling the preparation of food or for securing the observance of hygienic conditions and practices within commercial food operations. Only then can an order be made. The court must also be satisfied that the health risk condition is fulfilled with respect to the food business.

Proprietor (s 27(1)): is the person who carries on a food business.

Public analyst (s 27(1)): refers to persons who are appointed by any food authority in England and Wales and any regional or islands council within Scotland, to act as an analyst or analysts for the purposes of the Act. An appointment cannot be made unless that person possesses qualifications approved by the Minister or prescribed in regulations made by the Minister. If a person has a direct or even an indirect interest in a food business within a particular food authority's or council's area, he cannot act as a public analyst for that area.

Sale and related expressions (s 2): sale comprises an offer of sale, acceptance of that offer, and in England and Wales consideration given for that offer. Offer for sale must be distinguished from an invitation to treat. Sale is extended to include food supplied in the course of a business, otherwise than by a conventional sale as described above, and food offered as a prize or reward in connection with certain activities.

Common law exists to supplement the statutory provisions relating to the extension of the word "sale" and to the phrase "exposure for sale", a wider term used to cover situations not caught by "offer for sale". Thus an action may not constitute an offer for sale, but it will be classed as an exposure (*Keating v Horwood* (1926)).

Ship (s 53(1)): includes any vessel, boat or craft together with a hovercraft as defined by the Hovercraft Act 1968. Master of the ship is, consequently, taken to be the master of any of these things.

Slaughterhouse (s 53(1)): a place used for slaughtering animals whose flesh is intended for human consumption. It also includes lairages and other places for the keeping of animals prior to slaughter, and places available for use in connection with the slaughterhouse and which are used for keeping or subjecting to any process or treatment the products of slaughtered animals.

Substance (s 53(1)): includes the solid, liquid, gas or vapour state of any natural or artificial substance or other matter.

Treatment (s 53(1)): includes subjecting food to heat or cold.

Unfit for human consumption (s 8(4)): food which does not comply with one of the food safety requirements is that which is unfit for human consumption. In addition, in England and Wales it includes any product or part of a product obtained from an animal which has been slaughtered in a knacker's yard or obtained from a carcass taken into such a yard which is unfit. The same applies within Scotland to any product from an animal slaughtered otherwise than in a slaughterhouse.

Whether or not food is unfit is largely a question of fact, as has been illustrated by various common law decisions, and it is for the justices to decide in the final analysis. The phrase clearly covers food that is putrid or decomposed (*David Greig Ltd* v *Goldfinch* (1961)) but does not cover merely unsuitable cases (a stale loaf would be unsuitable but not unfit). Neither is it always necessary to prove the food injurious or dangerous (*Kyle* v *Laird* (1951)). Unfit can also extend to the situation where food contains extraneous material of a particular nature such as a dirty bandage within a loaf of bread (*Chibnalls Bakeries* v *Cope Brown* (1956)), but not metal in a cream bun or string in a slice of bread (*J Miller Ltd* v *Battersea Borough Council* (1956); *Turner and Son Ltd* v *Owen* (1956)).

Miscellaneous interpretations

In addition to interpretation of specific terms, s 53 provides that:

(i)   wherever mentioned "the 1984 Act" means the Food Act 1984, and "the 1956 Act" means the Food and Drugs (Scotland) Act 1956;

(ii)   the use of "regulations and orders made under the Act" refers to those made by the Minister or Ministers;

(iii)   a class or description within the Act can be created by referring to common matters or circumstances. In the case of a description of food, the matter which constitutes the description can be the brand name of the food as it is commonly sold;

(iv)   where the Act specifies time periods of less than seven days, and this period would include Saturday, Sunday, Christmas Day or a Bank Holiday, that day will not count as part of the seven-day period. Bank Holiday is one which is classed as such under the Banking and Financial Dealings Act 1971.

Chapter 3

The scope of the Act, food safety and consumer protection

The extent to which the Act applies is examined in the first part of this chapter, indicating the limitations of various provisions. In the following two sections the main provisions relating to food safety and consumer protection are discussed.

1. The scope of the Act

(a) Meaning of food (s 1)

To what extent the Act applies depends upon how wide the definition of food is taken to be. Since 1984 food expressly included drink, chewing gum and similar products together with articles and substances used as ingredients in the preparation of any of these things. It also expressly excluded water, live animals and birds, feeding stuff for animals, birds and fish, and drugs.

Food has been defined in its literal sense as what a person takes into the system to maintain life and growth (*Shorter Oxford English Dictionary*). Tied in with the definition is the word "preparation" which is taken to include manufacture and any form of processing. Thus it would seem that food incorporates anything consumed by humans to maintain life and growth, whether consumed alone or as potential ingredients such as baking powders, flavourings, colourings and condiments mixed with or added to other food before consumption. Of course the specific exclusions within any statute must be taken out of this definition of food.

Just how far the extension of the definition may be taken is illustrated by *Meah* v *Roberts; Lansley* v *Roberts* (1978). Here caustic soda solution mistakenly served for lemonade was held to be a sale of food. This followed the precedent set in *Knight* v *Bowers* (1885).

The literal interpretation of food and the volume of case law which serves to increase the scope of the definition of food are further supplemented by statutory provisions specifically including or failing to exclude certain things from the term.

As previously mentioned, the definition of food in s 1 of the Act expressly includes drink, chewing gum and similar products, with the catch-all phrase concerning articles and substances used as ingredients in the preparation of food or anything falling within the definition of food also remaining. A new inclusion in s 1 extends the scope of the Act by including within the definition of food articles and substances which have no nutritional value but are used for human consumption. This virtually ensures that "food", apart from the specific exemptions, includes anything which may be present in commodities normally consumed by humans.

Water now falls within the meaning of food (having been previously excluded by the Food Act 1984), and s 1 of the Act extends food safety provisions to this substance — a positive measure since water is an important feature in all food premises, businesses and concerns. When the Act was drafted, however, care was taken not to confuse responsibilities about the water supply to premises. It was then determined that responsibility for water up to the point of supply would remain with the water authority, whilst water used from the point of supply, classed as the tap point, would fall within the scope of the legislation relating to food safety.

By virtue of "drink" in s 1(1)(a), water is included within the definition of food, but the extent to which the Act applies is qualified by s 55 (water supplies: England and Wales) and s 56 (water supplies: Scotland). Essentially these sections prevent Part II of the Act, and any regulations or orders made under it, from applying to the water supply of any premises. Water supply is given the meaning of a supply of water provided by a water undertaker, including supply provided for the purposes of bottling water (s 60 Water Act 1989, s 3 Water (Scotland) Act 1980).

In terms of food safety, ss 55 and 56 ensure the application of water quality standards for domestic premises to water supplies used for food production purposes. Some quality standards are therefore now available to control water supplied for food production.

Water for food production purposes is defined by ss 55 and 56. This definition quite clearly states that food production purposes include the manufacture, processing, preservation or marketing of food or drink where water supplied to food production premises may be used in these operations. Food production premises are taken to be premises where a business of preparing food or drink for consumption off the premises is carried on. Quite obviously this does not include restaurants or cafes where food is consumed on the premises. This is due to the fact that water supplied to such premises is classed as water for domestic purposes — water quality standards for domestic premises apply and the quality of this water is therefore adequately controlled. In the past, water supplies at food factories have not fallen within this domestic purposes category and therefore the relevant water quality standards have not applied. The Act now provides for the extension of water supply quality controls to such processing units.

These controlling water quality provisions amend the Water Acts of England and Wales on the one hand, and of Scotland on the other hand, by the insertion of two new sections, ss 66 (1A) and 76L(1A) respectively.

Consequently, domestic water quality controls now apply to water supplied for food production purposes on food production premises up to the point of supply. After the point of supply water falls within the definition of food and is subject to control by the Act. The intention is that water as an important ingredient from the point of supply, should be brought under control by the food safety provisions whilst water supplies quite properly remain the responsibility of the water authority.

One other specific change is that the word "food" in s 1 of the Act does not now include living fish which are not used for human consumption whilst they remain alive. This distinction was never made in earlier legislation, although it ensures that any fish used in its live state for human consumption remains within the definition of food. If this were not so, then fish eaten live such as oysters would not be covered by the Act. This provision also ensures that live fish, such as trout and herrings, which are not used for human consumption until they are dead, remain protected by other more relevant statutory provisions. Quite logically the definition of food now attaches to fish when they are at the stage of being used for human consumption. For some this is when they are alive, for others it is not and this distinction is cleverly engineered by the phraseology "used for human consumption". Had "intended" been inserted instead of "used" then the whole subsection would have taken on a new meaning since even living fish can be "intended" for human consumption while alive.

The Act also expands upon the types of drugs which are not to be classed as food. Drugs not covered by s 1 are those which have been defined as controlled drugs by the Misuse of Drugs Act 1971. Medicinal products or other substances or articles subject to valid product licences required by order under ss 104 or 105 Medicines Act 1968 are also excluded. Where a product licence does exist, the Minister can make exceptions and, by order, provide that the particular product, article or substance is to be classed as food for the purposes of the Act. Any other drugs which do not fall within the controlled drug or product licence categories will be subject to control by the food safety provisions.

(b) Business, food business and food premises (s 1)

Section 1 also determines the extent to which key phrases of the Act apply. Business is stated to include canteens, clubs, schools, hospitals or institutions and public or local authority undertakings. The first five of these undertakings are included whether they are carried on for profit or not (s 1(3)), but in the case of public or local authorities the undertaking must be carried on for profit if it is to be classed as a business.

This is because in its literal sense business means a trade or commercial transaction which is carried on for profit or gain. Section 1 extends this to cover those five undertakings even when they are not run for a profit. However, by the very nature of the definition, public or local authorities are not afforded this extension so these undertakings, together with any others not listed within the five exceptions, must be carried on for profit to be covered by the term business. The extent of business has a major impact as to what may be considered food businesses and food premises since both hinge, albeit directly and indirectly, on the meaning of business. If an undertaking does not come within the above confines of the term "business" then any controls relating to food businesses do not apply since this phrase is defined as "any business in the course of which commercial operations with respect to food or food sources are carried out". Neither can the undertaking be classed as food premises as these are classed as any premises used for a food business.

Once the definition of business is satisfied, then both "food business" and "food premises" will apply to the undertaking provided that:

(i) commercial operations of the type listed in s 1(3) are carried out in the course of the food business; and

(ii) the definition of premises is satisfied. This is much wider than the type of premises envisaged by earlier legislation as it includes any place, vehicle, stall or movable structure.

This definition enables domestic premises which are being utilised as food businesses to be fully inspected and it is hoped that these will be more readily traced by enforcing authorities by means of a registration or licensing scheme. The whereabouts of food businesses operating from domestic premises has, in the past, been extremely difficult to establish and therefore control of the undertaking made difficult. Involvement by the authority has been more by chance, or as a result of the conscientious proprietor, or a report by a complainant.

On first impressions, the definition of premises appears to leave out ships and aircraft, with the implication that conveyances such as North Sea and cross-Channel ferries are no longer within the scope of the definition. This would also prevent the inspection of imported food carried as cargo. However, s 1(3) allows for an order to be made by the Minister which specifies certain ships and aircraft which are to be classed as premises for the purposes of the Act. Until the time that such an order is made s 59(3) by reference to Sch 4 ensures that "premises" includes home-going ships (as defined by s 132 Food Act 1984 and s 58 Food and Drugs (Scotland) Act 1956) and provides in addition that the powers of entry in s 32 of the Act will apply to ships and aircraft for the purposes of inspecting imported food where it is thought that a contravention of Part II of the Act exists.

These provisions of s 59(3) and Sch 4 are transitional in nature. They allow for the extension of the word "premises" and the powers of entry to continue in this way only until an order is made by the Minister under s 1(3). Once this order comes into force, the transitional provisions are no longer necessary.

At common law the use of the word premises has been curtailed in some instances. In *Grandi* v *Milburn* (1966) informations were laid against the company under s 1 Petroleum (Consolidation) Act 1928. These amounted to the company being an occupier of "premises", namely a petrol tanker on which petrol was kept without an authorising licence. It was held that there was no reason to extend the meaning of premises in s 1 of the Act beyond its ordinary and natural meaning. The ordinary and natural meaning of premises was taken to be land or buildings on land.

It is suggested that the extensive definition of premises in s 1 Food Safety Act will adequately cover most situations for what is not construed as a place, the concept of which requires something fixed (as in *Eldorado Ice Cream Co Ltd* v *Keating* (1938)), might be construed as a delivery vehicle (*Stone* v *Boreham* (1959)). If it is not a delivery vehicle, it may be a stall (*Greenwood* v *Whelan* (1967)). Furthermore, it is expected that case law will supplement the definition should it be shown to be defective in any way.

(c) Crown premises and immunity (s 54)

Not initially included within the scope of the Act or the definition of premises are those premises belonging to the Crown. The extension of food law to Crown premises, with the exception of premises relating to Her Majesty in her private capacity, is not expected until April 1992. (For the definition of Her Majesty in her private capacity see s 38(3) Crown Proceedings Act 1947.) Until s 54 is given full effect, all premises held or used by or on behalf of the Crown, such as prisons or Government offices, will remain immune from action under the Act.

This was the position under earlier legislation, supported at common law by *Bank voor Handel en Scheepvaart NV* v *Administrator of Hungarian Property* (1954). Such immunity also used to extend to the National Health Service and hospitals and buildings used by them, until the passing of the National Health Service (Amendment) Act 1986. The case of *Nottingham No 1 Area Hospital Management Committee* v *Owen* (1958) was regularly cited as authority for the decision to extend immunity to hospitals.

It was argued that hospitals were vested in the Ministry of Health by s 6 Ministry of Health Act 1919. As a result of s 7 of this Act the Minister of Health held the properties on behalf of the Crown. All hospital committees and management boards operated under the Minister's direction and therefore operated equally on behalf of the Crown. (This followed an earlier decision in *Cooper* v *Hawkins* (1904) where persons employed by the Crown were given the benefit of immunity.) Thus, in *Nottingham No 1 Area* it was held that the justices had no jurisdiction to hear complaint against a hospital management committee in respect of nuisance abatement as the premises and employees were protected by Crown immunity.

This was, and remains, good legal principle and therefore necessitated the passing of the 1986 Amendment Act. Following this piece of legislation, hospital kitchens became subject to the same requirements as other food premises. In 1988 a survey by the Institution of Environmental Health Officers indicated that only 20 per cent of hospitals visited had food handling areas that fell below the required regulatory standards, as compared with 42 per cent in 1987 and 48 per cent in 1986.

It is the objective of s 54 to secure the same vast improvement in other Crown premises. From the date of implementation these provisions and any associated relevant regulations and codes of practice will bind the Crown subject to special arrangements and certain exemptions. Although the Crown cannot be held criminally liable under the Act (s 54(2)), the enforcement authority will be able to apply to the High Court to declare unlawful any act or omission of the Crown. Section 54(3) ensures that *Cooper* v *Hawkins* is overruled by providing that persons in the public service of the Crown will be bound by the provisions of the legislation.

Where it is felt necessary in the interests of national security, the Secretary of State has the power to restrict entry to certain Crown premises (s 54(4)). Powers of entry are conferred by s 32, allowing an authorised officer of an enforcement authority to enter premises at all reasonable hours. In those circumstances where the Secretary of State feels that such a right to enter would endanger national security, he may issue a certificate naming the particular premises to which right of entry under s 32 may not be exercised. Once premises have been named in a certificate, an authorised officer will not have a right to demand entry – presumably any refusal of entry will not amount to the offence of obstructing an officer in the course of his duties. There is nothing to suggest that a pre-arranged visit will never be agreed to – it is the unexpected calling of an officer which gives cause for concern. Excessive use of this power by the Secretary of State could quite easily negate the usefulness of s 54; it is therefore hoped that powers of restricted entry are exercised only in relation to real cases of a threat to the nation's security.

(d) The extended meaning of sale

Throughout the Act it is apparent that "sale" of food is an important feature. In its ordinary sense sale must constitute an offer of sale, acceptance of that offer and consideration given for that offer – only then is there a legally binding contract. The aspect of consideration is not applicable in Scottish law of contract – any references to it are therefore purely in relation to England and Wales. In all other ways the law and provisions discussed apply equally to Scotland.

Any offer of sale must be distinguished from an invitation to treat as in *Partridge* v *Crittenden* (1968) where the placing of an advertisement in the "for sale" column of a periodical was held not to be an offer but an invitation to treat. In *Fisher* v *Bell* (1961) the display in a shop of an article with a price tag on it was held to be an invitation to treat. Once an offer has been made and accepted in England and Wales some consideration for the offer must be given; *Watson* v *Coupland* (1945) is authority for the proposition that sale depends upon the transfer of property. However, it is evident from *Thompson* v *Ball* (1948) that a real agreement to sell must also exist, and someone who is coerced into selling something is not always found to have "sold" that something for the purpose of food law.

Section 2 of the Act extends the ordinary meaning of sale to include food which is supplied in the course of business or which is offered as a prize even though no conventional sale or "offer for sale" actually took place. The phrase in s 2 (1)(a) of "the supply of food otherwise than on sale" has been used in earlier legislation and has attracted some discussion. Justices have tended to view "otherwise than on sale" very narrowly, restricting the extension of the meaning of sale merely because to widen it increases criminal liability. These words are designed to cover the case of the transfer of food to a person who intends to consume it but does not actually buy it or specifically give consideration for it.

In *Swain* v *Old Kentucky Restaurants Ltd* (1973) the extent to which s 2 of the Act will operate was made clear. The case concerned a restaurant customer who ordered a meal which included a jacket potato. On receiving his meal he found that the potato was bad inside. The potato was returned and the customer was not asked to pay for it – no actual sale having occurred or consideration given. Section 2 Food Act 1984 contained an offence for selling food not of the quality demanded, and information laid before the justices under s 2 was dismissed on the grounds that there had been no sale of food, as the customer had rejected the potato. On appeal to the divisional court it was held that the phrase "otherwise than by sale" in s 131(2) Food Act 1984 clearly provided that the supply of food in the course of business, otherwise than by sale, was deemed to be a sale of food – since this applied here, the case was returned to the justices with a direction to convict.

Any food not sold or offered for sale in the literal meaning of sale, but supplied in the course of a business, will be classed as a sale of food. So too will anything else which is specified in an order made by the Ministers under s 2(1)(b), a further possible way in which the meaning of sale may be extended.

The provisions of the Act also apply to food which is offered as a prize or reward, or given out as if that food had actually been exposed for sale. In respect of the latter, food must have been offered or given in connection with two activities. The first activity is any public entertainment, irrespective of whether or not the public is admitted to the entertainment by payment – admission itself is sufficient (*Buchanan* v *Motor Insurers' Bureau* (1955)). The Act itself gives the definition of entertainment as including social gatherings, amusements, exhibitions, performances, games, sports, or trials of skill. Secondly, food must have been offered or given for the purpose of advertisement or in furtherance of trade or business. The words "in furtherance" have been held to be wide enough to cover the advancement of something that is not yet in existence (*R* v *Tearse* [1945] 1 KB 1 at page 5 [1944] 2 All ER 403 at page 405).

Food exposed or deposited in any premises for the purposes of being offered or given away in connection with public entertainment, advertisement or furtherance of trade or business, will also be regarded as being exposed for sale. The term "exposure for sale" covers a much wider range of conduct than "offer for sale". In *Keating* v *Horwood* (1926) a baker delivering bread from an open car had completed his round and was returning to the bakehouse with some loaves still in his vehicle. On inspection one of these loaves was found to be deficient in weight and in subsequent proceedings the argument that the loaves were not exposed for sale was rejected. The principal reason for rejection was that once the journey had begun it was unclear which loaves, if any, would remain unsold, and those left would have been sold had any customers required them. Whilst they had not been offered for sale they had been exposed for that purpose.

To be exposed for sale, the goods themselves do not have to be seen – they can be completely hidden from view by a wrapper (*Wheat* v *Brown* (1892)), but exposure for view only is not exposure for sale (*Luke* v *Charles* (1861)). The term normally imports an intention to sell at the particular time of exposure so that it will not apply in respect of goods already sold, even if they have not yet been delivered (*Rye* v *Collip Ltd* (1957)).

(e) The use of statutory presumptions (s 3)

In order to assist the application and enforcement of the wider powers provided by the Act, its scope is increased by the existence of rebuttable, but none the less useful, statutory presumptions contained within s 3 upon which the prosecution may rely. They are aimed at pre-sale acts and are an attempt to assist the prosecuting authority in satisfying a court on the question of whether the food, articles or substances were intended for human consumption. Without these presumptions the burden of proving intention in some cases would be excessively heavy and the prosecuting local authority would have an almost impossible task in supplying the necessary evidence.

The presumption exists, until the contrary is proved, that the sale of any food was the sale of food for human consumption, and that any food offered or exposed or kept for sale was intended for sale for human consumption. Food for these purposes is taken to be food of a type commonly used for human consumption (s 3(2)).

Under s 3, food found on premises used for the preparation, storage or sale of food is presumed to have been intended for sale for human consumption; articles or substances found on such premises are presumed to have been intended to be used for the manufacture of food for human consumption.

Any food of a type commonly used for human consumption falls within s 3(2); articles and substances are interpreted as being of a kind commonly used in the manufacture of food for human consumption.

The last presumption concerns articles and substances used in the composition or preparation of any food commonly used for human consumption. If there are any such articles and substances found on premises where that food is prepared they shall be presumed to be for use in the composition or preparation for human consumption. All of these presumptions remain good until the contrary is proved, but "prove" does not mean beyond reasonable doubt (*per* Du Percy J in *Cant* v *Harlay* [1938] 2 All ER 768 at page 773). It is a lesser degree of proof that is required, more equatable to the balance of probabilities. The level of proof required for rebuttal has been shown to vary from case to case, although rebuttal is always possible provided that satisfactory evidence can be provided, as illustrated by *Hooper* v *Petrou* (1973). Here a restaurant proprietor was charged with having mice-infested pies in his possession which were for preparation for sale. The pies were in an inaccessible place in the storeroom and it was claimed that they were never meant for sale. However, the presumption of "intended for sale" existed. It was held on appeal to the Divisional Court that the presumption (as provided by s 98(2) Food Act 1984) was open to rebuttal either by evidence or, exceptionally, by the facts speaking strongly for themselves. In this case the rebuttal required evidence; since some of the defendant's evidence had not been heard it was difficult to imagine how the decision of the lower courts could have been conclusively made. The case was therefore remitted to a different bench for rehearing, with the possibility that the defendant's evidence might rebut the presumption of "intended for sale". Had the circumstantial evidence been more in favour of the defendant, evidence may not have been needed, with rebuttal of the presumption occurring automatically on the facts of the case.

(f) The Scilly Isles, Channel Islands, territorial waters and continental shelf (ss 57 and 58)

The Act was designed to regulate food law within England, Scotland and Wales. Under s 57 it is expressly extended to the Isles of Scilly, with any necessary amendments or modifications regarding its application being made by ministerial order. It is also possible for the Act to cover the Channel Islands once an Order in Council has been made by Her Majesty to direct this extension. Again, any modifications or exceptions or amendments necessary would be contained in the Order.

In an attempt to bring oil rigs and offshore installations under the Act, s 58 provides for application of the legal principles to such concerns as if they were part of the United Kingdom and situated specifically within it. This is achieved by all territorial water adjacent to Great Britain being deemed by s 58 to be part of Great Britain and therefore subject to the Act. Before the provisions can be applied, however, an Order in Council must be made directing that certain installations and offshore safety zones (as determined by Part III of the Petroleum Act 1987) in waters to which s 23 Oil and Gas (Enterprise) Act

1982 applies are to be treated, for the purposes of the Act, as part of Great Britain. This Order is made under s 23 of the 1982 Act which allows for the application of civil law to such installations, together with any necessary exceptions or modifications thought necessary.

Due to the special nature of this type of application, s 58 also makes provision for the practicalities of enforcing food safety legislation on installations of this type. Persons of "a specified description" as determined within the Order will be given the right to require transport to and from the installation for themselves and their equipment, together with the provision of reasonable accommodation and meals during their stay. Such rights will actually be conferred by the Order. References to food safety legislation include the Food Safety Act 1990 and any regulations made under it.

Again the extension of the Act in this sphere depends exclusively on the willingness of the Government to effect the appropriate Order in Council and to exercise restraint in including within the Order any exceptions or modifications to the legal provisions.

2. Food safety provisions (ss 7 – 13)

(a) Injurious to health

It is an offence to adulterate or process food for sale for human consumption in any way that renders it injurious to health (s 7). This section makes it illegal for any person to render food injurious to health by carrying out specified operations to it. These operations are the addition of any article or substance to the food, or their use as an ingredient in its preparation, the abstraction of any constituent from food and the processing or treatment of food. If any of these activities cause the food to become injurious to health, and that person intended that the food be sold for human consumption, then the offence is committed.

Person includes an employee of the proprietor of a business, as well as the proprietor himself (*Pearks, Gunston and Tee Ltd* v *Ward* (1902)), together with a body corporate (Sch 1 Interpretation Act 1978). A receiver who is carrying on the business is classed as "any person" and can be prosecuted

(*Meigh* v *Wickenden* (1942)). The emphasis is on the person who renders the food injurious and intends its sale for human consumption.

This section requires a positive action such as addition, abstraction, subjection or use, to be carried out to the food and does not therefore apply to food which has become injurious to health by decomposition. Abstraction may include failure to prevent the escape of an evanescent constituent (*Bridges* v *Griffen* (1925)) but does not include reducing the proportion of the constituent by dilution. This is an addition (*Dearden* v *Whiteley* (1916)). To constitute an offence it must be found as a fact that the end product has been rendered injurious to health. Where an ingredient which is injurious is added to the food it does not automatically follow that the food becomes injurious. The amount of injurious ingredient may be so small as not to change radically the food's composition (*Hull* v *Horsnell* (1904)). Neither is food injurious just because exceptional people are likely to be injured by it. Only where it affects a substantial portion of the community likely to use it can it be said to be injurious to health (*Cullen* v *McNair* (1908)). Proof of adulteration of the food is usually by an analyst's certificate. However, such a certificate is not essential to proceedings if other evidence of adulteration is available. The value of a certificate of analysis lies in the assessment of the potential or actual danger to health arising from the food concerned.

The section uses the word "article". In *Longhurst* v *Guildford, Godalming and District Water Board* (1961), Lord Reid commented that the word has many different meanings and therefore the context in which it appears is of crucial importance. The natural elements have been held to be "articles" (*Cox* v *S Cutler and Sons Ltd and Hampton Court Gas Co* (1948)), and only by express definition has electrical energy been excluded from the word by s 103(5) Factories Act 1937 − otherwise this would also have been considered an article.

Subsection (1) of s 7 does not create an absolute offence relating to the sale of food injurious to health; that is contained within s 8. Instead it requires intention that the food be sold for human consumption in that state. Proving intention is paramount for any proceedings to be successful under this provision. Adulterating food or allowing servants to do so with knowledge of their actions is also a misdemeanour at common law provided that the article of food was intended for sale for human consumption (*R* v *Macarty and Fordenbourgh* (1705)).

In determining whether food is injurious to health s 7(2) requires consideration of both the probable effects and the probable cumulative effects on the health of persons consuming the food in ordinary quantities. It is a continuation of previous provisions within the Food Act 1984 and Food and Drugs (Scotland) Act 1956. Cumulative effects are particularly important, bearing in mind the damage that some pesticides or heavy metals can do when taken into the human body over a period of time.

(b) Selling food

Various consumer associations have voiced the obvious concern that a general catch-all safety requirement has not been included with the food safety provisions. This would have ensured that all producers of food and, in fact, anyone involved in the food chain, would be placed under a duty to provide safe food. Instead of the general duty, a new provision exists that requires that food should not be sold unless it complies with the food safety requirements (s 8). These requirements are that the food should not be rendered injurious to health as defined by s 7, it should not be unfit for human consumption and it should not be so contaminated as to make its use for human consumption in that state unreasonable. As well as the sale of food for human consumption, s 8 makes it an offence for any person to offer, expose or advertise the sale of food for human consumption which does not meet the safety requirements. The possession for sale or for the preparation for sale of such injurious, unfit or contaminated food is also prohibited as is the deposition or consignment of the food to any other person for the purpose of sale or preparation for sale.

Under s 8(1)(a) it is an offence to offer or expose for sale food which does not meet the safety requirements. With reference to such types of provisions, *Watson* v *Coupland* (1945) is authority for the proposition that sale depends upon the transfer of property. An agreement to sell must also exist (*Thompson* v *Ball* (1948)) with coercion to sell being sometimes interpreted as no real agreement to sell. In some circumstances, since *Hotel Regina (Torquay) Ltd* v *Moon* (1940), a proprietor can be convicted in respect of sales by servants without his knowledge of the sales. Furthermore the time of payment within the transaction may be immaterial, with the relevant point being whether the transaction of sale in terms of acceptance of the offer was completed before it was disclosed that the food was in contravention of the legal provisions, rather than when the money changed hands.

The wording of this part of s 8 means that the section may indeed take account of today's hazards, but is not necessarily capable of applying to difficulties which may arise as a result of rapidly advancing food technology. A general safety duty would have overcome this possible inadequacy. Section 8 does, however, catch dangers that can occur accidentally, such as botulism, and therefore gives greater protection against contamination. It also applies to food within a factory as well as in a shop.

Contained within s 8(3) is a presumption that if any part of a batch of food does not comply with the food safety requirements, the whole batch is presumed not to comply unless the contrary is proven. The burden of proof is on the defendant and the degree of evidence must be sufficient to rebut the presumption.

(c) Powers to inspect and seize

For the purposes of "unfitness for human consumption", it is made clear that any part of an animal or product derived in whole or part from an animal which has been slaughtered at a knacker's yard, or whose carcass was brought into a knacker's yard, will be deemed to be unfit for human consumption. This maintains the line of control over knacker's yards. In Scotland such products or parts of an animal are classed as unfit for human consumption if the animal was not slaughtered within a slaughterhouse. The exception to this is where the animal is not slaughtered within a slaughterhouse because an accident, illness or emergency affecting the animal required it to be slaughtered elsewhere.

However, in such circumstances the inspection by the appropriate officer of the carcass and offal, can result in the officer deciding that these products are not fit for human consumption. Enforcement powers exist to inspect, seize and condemn food suspected of not complying with food safety requirements and to give notice that the food is not to be used for human consumption (s 9). This power to serve notice in relation to food that does not comply with food safety requirements is a new and useful addition, providing a useful reserve for preventing unsound food reaching the consumer.

The power to inspect food at all reasonable times applies to any food intended for human consumption which is sold, offered or exposed for sale, in the possession of any person or which has been deposited with or consigned to any person for the purpose of sale or for the preparation for sale. What is a reasonable time is a question of fact. The time during which the premises in question are open for business purposes is considered reasonable, and except in special circumstances an authorised officer would not be justified in demanding that the premises be opened at an unusual hour (*Small* v *Buckley* (1875)). Preventing the inspection of food by making it unavailable, perhaps in a locked cupboard, may also be considered as avoidance of the right "to inspect at all reasonable times" (*Davis* v *Winstanley* (1930)).

Where an authorised officer has inspected food as mentioned above and it appears to him that the food fails to comply with food safety requirements, he may do one of two things. He may give notice to the person in charge of the food that until the notice is withdrawn the food or any portion of it is not to be used for human consumption and that it is not to be removed except as directed within the notice. Any person contravening the provisions of this notice is guilty of an offence. An authorised officer may also serve such a notice in the above conditions where it appears to him, even though he has not carried out an inspection, that any food is likely to cause food poisoning or any disease communicable to human beings (s 9(2)).

As an alternative to giving notice the authorised officer can in both of the above circumstances seize the food and have it dealt with by a justice of the peace. Problems do occur as to what is meant by "seizure" of food, particularly where a large consignment of items is involved. In such cases a specimen of the consignment may be taken before the magistrate, if it is physically impossible to take all of it, and provided that the other is kept available for inspection this fulfils the condition of "having the food dealt with by the magistrates" (*Nello Simoni* v *Southwark Borough Council* (1956)).

It is important to remember that notice is given if food is seized on the basis of what "appears" to be non-compliance with the food safety requirements or a likely cause of food poisoning or communication of a disease to humans. Because a definite judgment has not been made at this stage, s 9(4) requires the authorised officer to determine whether or not the food does in fact comply with the safety requirements as soon as is reasonably practicable, and in any event within twenty-one days. If he determines that the safety requirement is satisfied, he must withdraw the notice at once; if it is not the case he must seize it and remove it so as to have it dealt with by a justice of the peace.

Where food is seized, the person in charge of it must be notified of the officer's intention to have it dealt with by a magistrate. The justice of the peace may then consider the appropriate evidence and decide whether or not the food contravenes the food safety requirements. If it does not, the justice will refuse to condemn the food and the food authority will be liable for compensation payable to the owner for any depreciation in the value of the food resulting from the seizure. Compensation is also due in the same terms if the authorised officer withdraws his notice served under s 9 because he determines within the twenty-one day period that the food does not contravene the food safety requirements. Any dispute regarding the amount of compensation payable is to be determined by arbitration (s 9(8)).

Should the justice decide that the food does contravene the safety requirements, he will condemn the food and order it to be destroyed or so disposed of as to prevent its use for human consumption. He will also order any reasonably incurred destruction or disposal expenses to be paid by the owner of the food (s 9(6)).

Where a person might be construed as guilty under s 7 or s 8 (rendering food injurious to health; sale of food not complying with the food safety requirements), he may take witnesses with him if he attends before the justice of the peace in respect of the seizure of food, and he is entitled to be heard.

In its application to Scotland, s 9(9) provides that any reference to a justice of the peace includes reference to the sheriff and to the magistrate, and that any court order requiring the destruction or disposal of food is sufficient evidence for proving that the food in question fails to comply with the food safety requirements. Any arbitration in Scotland will be by a single arbiter appointed by the sheriff.

Because s 8 extends the legislation to cover foodstuffs prepared or available for sale, enforcement officers will be able to prevent unsatisfactory food from being sold, a principle in keeping with the public interest.

(d) Improvement notices

Section 10 provides for the issuing of improvement notices where it is suspected that an offence under any relevant regulations has been committed. The use of these notices is consistent with the Health and Safety at Work etc Act 1974 and is a useful practical tool. If an authorised officer of an enforcement authority has reasonable grounds for believing that the proprietor of a food business is not complying with specified regulations, he may serve on that proprietor an improvement notice. These specified regulations are those which require, prohibit or regulate the use of any process or treatment in the preparation of food or those made for securing the observance of hygienic conditions and practices for commercial operations with respect to food or food sources.

The notice must state the officer's grounds for believing that there is a contravention, and must specify the matters that constitute the failure to comply. It must also give the measures which the officer believes will ensure compliance, and require them to be completed within a specified time. Any time specified must be in excess of fourteen days.

(e) Prohibition orders

Prohibition orders preventing a certain activity or use are available under the Act by virtue of s 11. The application of these orders depends upon the health risk condition being fulfilled. This is essentially fulfilled where the use for any food business of any process, treatment or equipment and the construction of any premises or the state or condition of any premises or equipment used for the purposes of the business, involves a risk of injury to health. When it is found that this risk of injury exists and the court is satisfied that the proprietor of that food business has been convicted of an offence under regulations of a type specified in s 10 (improvement notices), the court has the power to issue the appropriate prohibition.

The appropriate prohibition will concern one of three things:

  (i) a prohibition on the use of a process or treatment within the business which involves a risk of injury to health;

 (ii) a prohibition on the use of premises or equipment for the purposes of that business or any other food business in that class or description, where their construction or use involves a risk of injury to health;

(iii) a prohibition on the use of premises or equipment for the business where their state or condition involves a risk of injury to health.

The court's ability to prohibit the use of a process or treatment for the purpose of a business or to prohibit the whole premises being used as a food business is an advancement and should be welcomed. It is essential where there is a necessity to safeguard public health that the courts use this power, especially since prohibitions do not have to cover the entire premises but may be placed on specific processes or equipment.

In some cases the prohibition may be placed on the proprietor of a food business who is convicted of an offence under regulations specified in s 10 as mentioned above; if the court, upon consideration of all the circumstances, thinks it proper, an order preventing that proprietor taking part in the management of any particular food business can be made. The order can also specify a class or description of food business to which this personal prohibition extends (s 11(4)).

Once an order has been made by the court under s 11, the enforcement authority must serve a copy of the order on the proprietor of the business as soon as is practicable. When the appropriate prohibition relates to processes, treatments, premises or equipment, a copy of the order must also be placed on premises used for the business in question. This must be placed in a conspicuous position.

Contravention of any order is an offence.

Any order, although made by the court, is served by the local authority and lifted by it when the risk of injury to health is removed. The order ceases to have effect when the enforcement authority issues a certificate stating that it is satisfied that the risk of injury has been removed and therefore the health risk condition is no longer fulfilled (s 11(6)). This certificate must be issued within three days of the authority being satisfied that the risk of injury no longer exists, and within fourteen days of application for the certificate by the proprietor. If the enforcement authority receives any application for a certificate, and it determines that it is not satisfied that the risk has abated, then it must give the proprietor its reasons.

An order containing a prohibition preventing the proprietor from participating in the management of a food business can be removed only by the court giving direction to this effect (s 11(6)(b)). This direction is only forthcoming where the proprietor makes an application to the court at least six months after the prohibition was imposed by order, or at least three months after he last applied for the direction. If the court finds from the evidence provided that the proprietor's conduct since the making of the order is satisfactory, and all other circumstances are favourable, it will make the direction to the local authority to lift the order.

Section 11(10) extends the term "proprietor of the business" to include the "manager of a food business" for the purposes of imposing the appropriate prohibition in relation to management. Thus a manager, being any person entrusted by the proprietor with the day-to-day running of the business, or any part of it, can in the same way as the proprietor be prevented from taking part in the management of food businesses in certain circumstances.

This is a useful protective element of the Act in that it allows the enforcement officer to reach the exact nerve centre of the problem. Premises can be up to date, technically sound and fully equipped, but the management and procedural aspect may still give cause for concern. Removal of bad management in the most difficult of cases can secure an instant improvement.

Section 11 also applies where an emergency prohibition order has been made under s 12(2). If the magistrates' court or sheriff (in Scotland) makes an emergency prohibition order, this is classed as if a proprietor of a food business has been convicted of an offence under regulation (s 11(1)).

(f) Emergency prohibition powers

Where an imminent risk of injury to health exists, as opposed to a risk of injury in s 11, emergency prohibition powers exist allowing enforcement authorities to impose prohibitions at very short notice. The ability to prohibit immediately any process or practice, including the carrying on of the business, where there is a risk to health is a great addition to enforcement powers. The authorised officer again has to be satisfied that the health risk condition is fulfilled with respect to the food business – the same criteria apply as in s 11, although risk of injury is not enough. For s 12 it must be an imminent risk of injury. Once he is satisfied of imminent risk of injury, he may serve on the proprietor of the business an emergency prohibition notice which imposes the appropriate prohibition. The appropriate prohibition can be the stopping of any process or treatment being carried out, or stopping the use of any premises or equipment in connection with a food business. The officer must, as soon as practicable after serving this notice, fix a copy of it on the premises used for the business (s 12(5)). It is then necessary for an emergency prohibition order to be obtained from the court. The proprietor must be notified of the authorised officer's intention to apply to the court for an emergency prohibition order, and this notice must be given at least one day before the date of the application. Furthermore, application to the court must be within three days of the service of the emergency prohibition notice.

If application for the order is not made within three days, the notice ceases to have effect. It also becomes ineffective as soon as an application for the order is accepted or refused (s 12(7)). If the notice ceases to have effect because of non-compliance with the three day rule, or because the court will not accept the application for, and thus grant, the emergency prohibition order since it feels that the health risk condition was not fulfilled at the time the notice was served, the local authority will be liable to pay compensation to the proprietor. This will be in respect of any loss suffered by the proprietor due to his compliance with the notice. The justice of this is obvious, with any disagreement as to the amount of compensation due being dealt with by arbitration in England and Wales, and by a single arbitrator appointed by the sheriff in Scotland.

Once application for an order is made within the time allowed, and the magistrates' court or sheriff (in Scotland) determines that the health risk condition was fulfilled when the notice was served, the appropriate prohibition will be imposed by order.

Contravention of any notice or order by any person is an offence. As with s 12, the enforcement authority must issue a certificate stating that it is satisfied that the proprietor has removed the imminent risk to health within three days of its being so satisfied. If the proprietor applies for this certificate, the enforcement authority must decide as soon as is reasonable, and at the most within fourteen days, whether the health risk condition is still satisfied or not. If it accepts that it is not satisfied, it must issue the certificate removing the notice or order. If the risk condition is still satisfied, the proprietor must be given reasons as to why the enforcement authority still considers there to be an imminent risk to health.

Power to serve improvement and prohibition notices is a new and useful concept in food law, but it has already been in existence under health and safety law. From the use of these notices for health and safety purposes it is clear that a properly drafted improvement notice must not merely state that in the opinion of the officer a contravention has occurred. The notice should identify the contravention by reference to the particular section and subsection − if the contravention is not so identifiable, particulars of it should be given (*West Bromwich Building Society* v *Townsend* (1983)). Since person includes body corporate as well as an individual (s 5 and Sch 1 Interpretation Act 1978) the notice must be addressed to whichever one is committing the offence. Consequently a notice addressed to a person employed in the food business rather than to the proprietor himself may be invalid if it alleges breach of a statutory duty imposed on the proprietor and not on the person (*Naylis* v *Manners* (1978)).

Section 37 (1)(a) provides for an appeal to the magistrates' court or sheriff (in Scotland) against the decision of an authorised officer of an enforcement authority to serve an improvement notice. (Note that here appeal is not to a tribunal.) Upon an appeal being lodged, the court has the power under s 39 to either cancel or affirm the notice. If the court agrees with the notice it may affirm it either as it is presented or with any modifications it thinks necessary.

The provisions of ss 10–12 will enable officers to ensure that food in the chain is safe, as well as to ensure that food premises comply with standards relating to construction or repair. The concept of notices detailing works necessary to ensure that risks to health are removed in a specified time ensures compliance without the prospect of bottlenecks in the courts. Of course, cases will go to court if notices are not complied with and also where an imminent risk to health exists with possible closure of the premises being likely. But the options now available of informal action, notice, order or prosecution mean that the enforcing authority has a much wider discretion as to the severity with which the law is applied. In the past minor difficulties which required a remedy were often not initially serious enough to warrant legal action and had to be dealt with on an informal basis. Now improvement notices, prohibition notices or orders and emergency prohibition orders may be used depending upon the circumstances. The ability to close premises immediately, albeit with confirmation via the court, will ensure that public safety is protected.

(g) Emergency control orders

The final provision relating to food safety is the power to make emergency control orders which may prohibit commercial operations in relation to food, food sources or contact materials when there is an imminent risk of injury to health. Under the old legislation controls could only be applied to specific geographical areas, a difficult and time-consuming concept if food had been distributed to many outlets. Hence the new controls were introduced to stop, for example, irradiation, processing of lead-contaminated meat and so forth. At the discretion of the Minister, an order can be made prohibiting the carrying out of commercial operations with respect to food, food sources or contact materials of any class or description. The only requirement is that these commercial operations involve or may involve imminent risk of injury to health (s 13(1)). Contravention of the order is an offence although the Minister may consent to the carrying out of certain prohibited things – the consent may or may not have conditions attached to it as required (s 13(3)). The defence to an offence of contravening an emergency control order is that consent had been given under subs (3) and that all imposed conditions had been complied with.

In addition to the order and to ensure compliance with the prohibition, s 13(5) allows the Minister to give directions preventing commercial operations. These directions may relate to food, food sources or contact materials which are believed to be subject to the emergency control order. The Minister has only to believe on reasonable grounds that the food, food sources or food contact materials are the subject matter of the order. It is important to note that they do not actually have to be controlled by it. He is also empowered by s 13 (5)(b) to do anything else which appears necessary to ensure that the emergency control order is complied with and that certain commercial operations are prevented. Failure to comply with a direction is an offence. The Minister may also recover all reasonable expenses accrued from actions by him in respect of a person not complying with an emergency order.

These stronger powers are welcomed by enforcement officers and are seen as the means of ensuring effective application of the law.

(h) Audit Commission survey

It is also intended that more even enforcement standards and a wider adoption of good practice will be promoted by the use of the legal provisions contained within ss 7–13. The need for these increased controls over the food industry was highlighted by the Audit Commission survey published in June 1990.

In April 1990 a national Food Premises Condition Survey was organised by the Audit Commission in co-operation with the Institution of Environmental Health Officers. Over 5,000 premises were inspected by environmental health officers (EHOs) in nearly 300 local authorities in England and Wales. Based on random selection, a sample of local authorities representative of regions and classes of authority was taken. Types of food premises were drawn from the rating list of each local authority. Standard survey forms were used in an attempt to achieve consistency, with the EHO being required to inspect the chosen premises within his authority and to make an assessment of health risk of the premises generally, as well as in terms of a number of factors under three general headings: training and hygiene awareness, equipment and practices. Each of the premises visited was evaluated in terms of the health risks found and four "risk" categories were available: negligible, minor, significant and imminent risk.

Negligible risk denoted premises where the health risk presented little or no danger to the public, even though improvements in food handling might be possible. The minor risk category was applied where some small risk to health was evident, with the necessary improvements being straight-forward and not of an urgent nature. In premises where the health risk was such as to cause serious concern with prompt action being necessary, a significant risk assessment was made; finally, imminent risk applied to premises where the risk to health was severe and immediate and urgent action was required − such as a situation involving contaminated food.

The results of the survey suggested that in almost one in eight food premises in England and Wales a significant or imminent health risk existed, and that one-third of these should be prosecuted or closed down. Inadequate temperature control of stored food, non-existent or unsatisfactory hand-washing facilities, cross-contamination of food and low priority given by management to safety were the major problems encountered. The findings also illustrated two other things: that overall risk increased as the time since the last inspection increased, a direct indication of the lack of qualified EHOs, and that a link existed between good training and lower health risk.

(i) Summary

It is evident that the food safety provisions provide improved enforcement powers to combat the obvious unsatisfactory situation within the food industry. So, too, do the requirements of subordinate legislation made under ss 16–19, discussed at the end of this chapter, with draft temperature control provisions and detailed training requirements already underway. These stronger food safety constraints require more intensive enforcement and therefore extra staff will be needed to carry out the new duties effectively. Additional resources necessary in terms of funding increased manpower have to be available. The Government appeared to have taken this into account when steering the Bill through its various stages with an extra £30m having been made available for 1991/92 via the Revenue Support Grant Supplement. The method of allocation to the various local authorities, and the extent to which the enforcement duties have increased due to the Act, will determine whether or not this figure is adequate.

3. Consumer protection (ss 14 and 15)

Two sections provide the basis for consumer protection. Section 14 makes it an offence to sell food which is not of the nature, substance or quality demanded by the purchaser and s 15 creates an offence of falsely or misleadingly labelling, describing, advertising or presenting food. This food must be for the purpose of sale or be in the possession of someone for the purpose of sale.

Section 14 is a direct transcript of the old s 2 Food Act 1984 and contains references to a sale which is to the prejudice of the purchaser. The offences created by such a provision are the foundations of food law within the United Kingdom and have been by far the most frequently used in proceedings. Where the facts of a case concern product descriptions, proceedings may be brought under the Trade Descriptions Act 1968 and consequently the provisions of s 18 Interpretation Act 1978 should be remembered:

"where an act or omission constitutes an offence under two or more Acts or both under an Act and at common law, the offender shall unless the contrary intention appears, be liable to be prosecuted and punished under either or any of these Acts or at common law, but shall not be liable to be punished more than once for the same offence".

Where s 14 is used, the effective *de minimis* requirement must also be considered in that only sales which were to the prejudice of the purchaser should be subject to redress. In *Smedleys Ltd* v *Breed* (1974) Viscount Dilhorne stated "Where it is apparent that a prosecution does not serve the general interests of consumers, the justices may think fit, if the Act has been contravened, to grant an absolute discharge".

The way in which nature, substance or quality is determined can be by analysis, and as for the other provisions relating to food safety regulations and description or presentation of food, the sampling and analysis procedures are as determined by ss 29–31 of the Act, discussed in Chapter 4.

Under s 14 there appears to be no need to prove intent to sell (*Pain* v *Boughtwood* (1890)) although there has to be an agreement to sell. In *Thompson* v *Ball* (1948) a licensee refused twice to sell adulterated whisky but in fear of the offence of obstruction he sold it on a third request to a sampling officer. It was held that a sale to the prejudice of the purchaser had not taken place as there had never been a real agreement to sell.

With regard to the meaning of the word "prejudice" in the context of the section, two propositions have been established. The first is that if the purchaser is given notice that the subject matter of the sale is not of the nature, substance or quality demanded, and this notice is given before the agreement to sell is concluded, then there is no prejudice to the purchaser. Secondly, the subject matter may be to the purchaser's prejudice even without proof that he actually sustained prejudice or damage. Where notice is given, it is necessary to prove that notice has been given to the purchaser (*Preston* v *Grant* (1925)). Once this has been done, sufficiency of that notice is considered and in *Sandys* v *Small* (1878) sufficiency was held to be a question of fact. It clearly is not necessary to disclose what the discrepancy actually is (*Williams* v *Friend* (1912)); but the substance of the information given to the purchaser must be adequate, as must the steps taken to convey this information to the average purchaser (*Rodburn* v *Hudson* (1925)) – the "average purchaser" being an objective test rather than a subjective assessment of the actual purchaser. The substance of the information is a question of law in that the purchaser must be told in substance that the thing which he is getting is not the thing for which he asked. Conveyance of the information to the actual purchaser is a question of fact and for the justices to decide in each case, with *Pearks, Gunston and Tee Ltd* v *Ward* (1902) holding that the question is what would be the position, not of a skilled purchaser like an inspector, but of an ordinary person purchasing the article without special knowledge. However, where a person does buy food not of the nature, substance or quality demanded for analysis or examination, s 14(2) ensures that an offence is still committed as it states that it shall be no defence to say that the purchaser was not prejudiced because he bought the food for such purposes.

The second proposition with regard to the construction of the word "prejudice" in s 14 is that it is not necessary to prove actual damage to the purchaser. In *Hoyle* v *Hitchman* (1879) prejudice was held to mean that which is suffered by anyone who pays for one thing and gets another of inferior quality. Furthermore it was stated in this case that the "prejudice of the purchaser" was necessarily included because, if it had not been so inserted, a person might have received a superior article which he demanded and paid for – yet still an offence would have been committed as it was not of the nature, substance or quality demanded.

When using s 14, it is necessary to decide in each case which of the three words, nature, substance or quality is most appropriate. The use of more than one word in the laying of information would allege more than one offence and would make the information bad for uncertainty (Magistrates' Courts Rules 1981 r 12). It is submitted that "nature" applies to things sold which are not of the variety or kind asked for, as where whiting is sold as hake. For articles containing foreign bodies or mould or having some adulterant added, or not containing the proper ingredients, "substance" is perhaps the most appropriate word to use – although in many instances "quality" would also be applicable. "Quality" is used where an article falls short of that expected by the ordinary buyer, or contains a lesser amount of an ingredient which is required by regulations. In many cases, however, regulations imposing such standards also contain the offence – use of this or s 14 will have to be considered in the circumstances.

"Substance" is frequently used in cases of milk containing antibiotic residues or other foods containing pesticide residues, but the presence of a foreign body in food which is sterile and harmless and not affecting the substance of the food does not necessarily constitute an offence under substance even though the foreign body is not of the substance of the food (*Edwards* v *Llaethdy Meirion Ltd* (1957)). But if the extraneous matter could be dangerous, the position must be distinguished from the principle in this case. Thus in *Southworth* v *Whitewell Dairies Ltd* (1958) milk with a sliver of glass in it was held to be to the prejudice of the purchaser and not of the substance demanded. It was held in *Anness* v *Grivell* (1915) that "quality" meant commercial quality having regard to any statutory standards of composition of the food in question and not merely description. The presence of a foreign body in food can make the food not of the quality demanded (*Newton* v *West Vale Creamery Co Ltd* (1956)), such as a housefly in a bottle of milk, or indeed a straw (*Barber* v *Co-operative Wholesale Society Ltd* (1983)).

When a purchaser asks for a particular food, the food "demanded" for the purpose of the section is the food known commercially under the name used. The question of what was demanded, as in what was actually said by the purchaser, is again a question of fact for the justices (*per* Grove J in *Pashler* v *Stevenitt* (1876)), and if there is room for debate as to the meaning of a description, the court will take into account what is generally understood by the trade and the public. Thus in *Sandys* v *Rhodes* (1903) a grocer was charged with selling a variety of tapioca as sago. The justices found that the two cost very much the same, and that the trade and the public generally knew as sago the substance sold, and therefore no offence had been committed. Where, however, there is an obvious disparity between the purchaser's description and the article supplied, such as margarine sold for butter, chicory for coffee, or as in *Knight* v *Bowers* (1885) savin for saffron, an offence is committed under this section.

If an opinion of an expert, such as a public analyst, is disputed, such evidence is not enough in itself to justify a conviction; it is necessary to provide evidence that a member of the public would have expected something different from that sold. But if the public analyst's opinion is undisputed and it is to the effect that the article is not as demanded, the court should convict (*Williams* v *Hurrells Stores Ltd* (1954)).

The existence of a statutory standard has a bearing on whether the quality is that demanded. If food is not of the statutory standard, an offence has been committed. If there is no statutory standard, the justices must fix a standard for themselves as a matter of fact to be decided on the evidence (*Roberts* v *Leeming* (1905) (margarine); *Wilson and McPhee* v *Wilson* (1903) (brandy); and *Preston* v *Jackson* (1928) (vinegar)).

The cases of *Goldup* v *Manson* (1982) and *Lawrence* v *Burleigh* (1981) are of great importance in respect of foods for which there is no statutory standard and where there is no standard stated or implied by way of a label, description, notice or otherwise.

The question to be considered by the court in both cases was whether the purchaser received an article of the quality which, under the relevant transaction, he was entitled to expect. In each case it was a question of fact as no statutory standard existed to guide the court.

The *Goldup* case concerned the purchase of cheap minced beef which was found to have 33 per cent fat content. More expensive mince was available at a different price. A notice was present in the shop which stated that minced beef sold there had up to 30 per cent fat. The defendants were charged with selling, to the prejudice of a purchaser, food which was not of the quality demanded by him. The purchaser was a sampling officer. Samples obtained by the prosecution analyst were found to have less than 25 per cent fat within them, and the analyst indicated that minced beef should not have more than 25 per cent fat. However, the price of these samples was not submitted in evidence − nor was it submitted as to whether the samples were taken from the cheap or expensive minced beef.

The magistrate acquitted the defendants, holding that the price at which minced beef was sold was crucial in determining the quality demanded by the purchaser when there was no statutory standard in existence.

Furthermore, in view of the price of the cheap minced beef, it was not proven beyond reasonable doubt that the mince sold at that price and which contained 33 per cent fat was not of the quality demanded by the purchaser.

The prosecutor appealed contending that where the standard of food was not prescribed, the magistrates were required to find a standard and could do so only on the evidence before them. Thus where, as in this case, expert evidence as to an appropriate standard was available, the magistrates should accept that evidence and act upon it. This appeal was dismissed on two counts.

The first was that since the analyst's evidence did not indicate the price of the samples obtained, or whether they were the cheap or expensive variety, but was merely a bare statement of opinion, then his evidence was not evidence of the quality demanded by the purchaser. Bare opinion of an expert witness as to a standard would not constitute such evidence since the standard of the "quality" of food was defined within the statute (s 2(1) Food and Drugs Act 1955) in terms of the quality demanded by the purchaser and not in terms of a prescribed or statutory standard. The quality demanded was therefore determined by implication or inference from all the surrounding circumstances, and the expert's standard was not evidence of and could not be substituted for the standard demanded by the purchaser. Secondly, in view of the notice within the shop stating that the minced beef's maximum fat content was 30 per cent, the purchaser selecting the cheaper brand impliedly asked for mince containing fat up to this amount; the 3 per cent excess fat present in the purchased sample was minimal and did not operate "to the prejudice of the purchaser".

The *Lawrence* case was much simpler. Here minced beef was sold over the telephone; investigations revealed from analysis of the meat delivered that it contained 30.8 per cent fat. Similar proceedings based on like offences in the *Goldup* case were instigated. The magistrates convicted and the company appealed.

In his judgment Ormrod LJ stated that it was for the magistrates to determine as a question of fact, whether or not the food was of the quality demanded. In some cases this standard would be less than 30 per cent, and in other cases more. The question was whether the purchaser was prejudiced, and in this case the most impressive evidence was from the purchaser herself. She was experienced in buying minced beef, a regular customer at the shop and when she saw the mince she did not believe it to be of the quality she reasonably expected. The analyst had given evidence to illustrate that the fat content was high, and that he had much experience in the analysis of mince samples generally. The court thought that the magistrates were right to put together the buyer's evidence and that of the analyst, and to reach the conclusion that they did. The magistrates quite rightly had asked themselves if, with there being no fixed standard, it was for them to fix the proper standard on the evidence before them. Consistent with the *Goldup* case, they had decided that it was; as a guide to the proper standard, they had considered all circumstances of the particular case, and had concluded correctly that the proper standard had not been met.

From these two cases can be extracted points which may be of assistance in understanding the basis of "quality demanded" in the absence of a fixed statutory standard:

(a) *evidence of prejudice*: the evidence of the purchaser as to personal prejudice in the *Lawrence* case was of considerable influence on the court. In the *Goldup* case the purchaser was a sampling officer and although it would have been no defence to allege that he was not prejudiced, he gave no evidence of prejudice and could not have done so;

(b) *notice given to the buyer as to quality*: in the *Goldup* case, at the time of the purchase by the sampling officer there was a notice in the shop which stated that minced beef contained up to 30 per cent fat. No such notice was given in the *Lawrence* case;

(c) *the evidence of the analyst*: it is possible in such cases where no statutory standard exists to rebut the observations of the public analyst;

(d) *the price*: the acquittal in the *Goldup* case depended, to some extent, on two qualities of mince being available at different prices. Thus the price can be an important factor in the determination of prejudice. However, this applies only where there is more than one price.

Section 14 (2) provides that any reference to sale within s 14(1) should be construed as a sale for human consumption.

The description and presentation of food are controlled by s 15. Here an offence is committed if any person sells food with a label, whether or not it is attached to or printed on the food's wrapper or container, which falsely describes the food or is likely to mislead as to the nature, substance or quality of the food.

Not only is it an offence in respect of any food sold, but it also applies with respect to any food offered or exposed for sale or in the person's possession for the purpose of sale. References to sale are construed as references to sale for human consumption (s 15(5)).

Where labelling of the food is not involved, yet an advertisement is published which falsely describes food or is likely to mislead as to the nature or substance or quality of the food, an offence is committed by the publisher or any person involved in publication (s 15 (2)).

"Falsely describes food" refers to an explicit false description on the label. Cases of oral misdescription are therefore not relevant in this context. Guidance can, however, be obtained from cases of written false trade descriptions under the Trade Descriptions Act 1968. Section 3 (1) of this Act states that a false trades description is one which is false to a material degree. It is no defence to prove that the falsely described article is as good as it purports to be. In *Kirbenboim* v *Salmon and Gluckstein* (1988), a case concerning cigarettes described as "hand-made" but which were machine-made, the description was held to have been intended to deceive, although the cigarettes were of the same quality paper, starch and tobacco as hand-made cigarettes.

"Likely to mislead" stems from the case of *McDowell* v *Standard Oil Co (New Jersey)* (1927) where it was held that "intended to mislead" (part of the old legislation relating to false descriptions of food in s 6 Food Act 1984) meant "likely to mislead". The distinction between a false description and a misleading one can be narrow. A false statement may be false on account of what it omits, even though it is literally true (*R* v *Lord Kylsant* (1932) and *Curtis* v *Chemical Cleaning and Dyeing Company Ltd* (1951)). Nevertheless, as a working rule it is submitted that the safe course is to allege that the label is false if there is a clear factual misstatement, and to allege that it is misleading if the label is false only by inferring or omitting something of importance.

With respect to the words "publishes" and "publication" it must be observed that these words are used in relation to an advertisement which includes any "notice, circular, label, wrapper or other document and any public announcement made orally or by means of transmitting light or sound". It seems that a person would not be party to a publication who neither knew of it nor assented to it, nor received any benefit from it, nor took part in it in any way (*Thorne* v *Heard and Marsh* [1895] AC 495 at page 503).

Section 15 includes two other provisions. The first is an offence of presenting food in a way which is likely to mislead as to the nature, substance or quality. This food has to be sold, offered or exposed for sale or in the person's possession for sale before it is caught by the provision. It is aimed at the pre-sale act of presentation of food. The second is where the label or advertisement mentioned in s 15(1) and (2) contained an accurate description of the composition of food. Even though this may have been the case, the court may still find that an offence has been committed. Accurate compositional values given on the label or in the advertisement do not provide an outright defence to proceedings where it is felt that other aspects of the information given are in contravention of s 15.

Chapter 4

Regulations, codes of practice and defences

An appraisal of subordinate legislation provided for by the Act is made within this chapter, completing the analysis of the legislative requirements contained within the new statute. The availability of defences to certain actions arising under the Act and associated regulations is also discussed.

1. Regulations under s 16 and Sch 1

The first enabling section is s 16 which, when read together with Sch 1, allows the Minister to make regulations for a wide range of food safety measures. The Act is designed to cover on a general basis all food caught within the definition of this term and to ensure the application of important provisions, such as rendering food injurious to health and selling food not complying with the food safety requirements. The Act does not lay down detailed requirements for the treatment of foods, or processes or compositional standards or any other such entities. Such in-depth requirements were intended to be contained within specific regulations supplemented by codes of practice suggesting methods for compliance with the regulatory controls. Note that codes of practice do not have the force of law; any deviation, however, from the method illustrated within the code is a *prima facie* case against any defendant who has been charged with an offence under the Act. To discharge the case against him, the defendant will have to show that he followed a method equally acceptable as that contained within the code of practice.

All references to food within s 16 and Sch 1 are intended to be in relation to food intended for sale for human consumption. Any reference to food source is in relation to a source from which food intended for human consumption is derived (s 16(5)).

Section 16 gives the general subject matter of the regulations which can be made under it, while Schedule 1 lists provisions which can be contained within these regulations. These two enabling measures allow the implementation of a comprehensive range of food safety and consumer protection measures designed to protect and safeguard the public. To ensure such protection, it is important that a whole package of safety provisions is developed as soon as possible so that they can be laid before Parliament and come into force with the main sections of the Act.

A summary of the various regulations and provisions available under s 16 is given below.

(a) Regulations for the composition of food

The Minister may choose to implement regulations for requiring, prohibiting or regulating certain specified substances within food or food sources. In addition, the general regulation of the composition of food is provided for.

This ensures adequate control of the constituents of food, and may be achieved by the use of provisions which prohibit or regulate the sale or possession of any substance which is to be used in the preparation of food. "Sale" includes possession for sale, offer, exposure or advertisement for sale − and the substance or its class must be specified. The regulation of the possession of any specified substance for use in food preparation is an obvious attempt to control pre-sale acts at the very beginning of the food processing chain, thus giving greater powers to the enforcement authority.

(b) Ensuring that food is fit for human consumption

This may be by the introduction of microbiological standards, a useful notion especially in the case of cooked meats and other pre-cooked products. Once food is declared not to comply with any of the standards laid down by regulation, it will be deemed to be unfit for human consumption. Section 8 and related offences under the Act will then apply to this food. This is an excellent example of how regulations contain the detailed requirements, while the Act provides the basic controls.

One area of concern is that any microbiological standards set should not provide an absolute minimum level to which the food industry will adhere. The promotion of the highest possible standards for food safety is essential.

The way in which regulations of this nature would provide adequate control falls into a number of categories. Food which has been derived from a food source which has been suffering from, has suffered from or is likely to suffer from a disease listed in the regulations will be restricted in sale. It will be an offence to sell any food of this nature for human consumption or to use it in the manufacture of products for sale for this consumption. A similar provision will also exist for shellfish taken from layings designated by the regulations.

These types of requirements essentially begin the control at the source of the food. If the source is suspect, food derived from it will not be allowed into the food chain.

So as to prevent food which is unfit from re-entering the chain, provision for regulating the treatment and disposal of any unfit food must be available. It is envisaged that this regulation will extend to food which is not unfit but which is not intended for, or is prohibited from being sold for, human consumption. Current methods of treatment include sterilisation of foodstuffs, especially meat, and any new regulations will include, by virtue of Sch 1, the power for enforcement authorities to register premises used for the sterilisation of meat. The use of premises not registered in accordance with such regulations will be an offence. Should the Minister think it necessary, a licensing system in respect of sterilisation premises can also be invoked.

(c) Processing and treatment of food

It is necessary to ensure the regulation of any process or treatment in the preparation of food. After any of these actions, food must remain within the legal parameters set down by the Act. It is possible for the Minister to prohibit or regulate the use of any process or treatment in the preparation of food, and in some instances to demand its use. This can be achieved by a licensing system whereby a licence issued by an enforcement authority can either allow or prohibit the use of any process or treatment. This will be particularly useful in the case of unknown practices.

However, to give a balanced situation, the Minister can consider the written opinions of relevant persons regarding the use of any process or treatment. Such relevant persons should possess qualifications prescribed by any regulations; it is possible for certain actions to be prohibited on the basis of these opinions. New technological or other processes or treatments can thus be fairly considered in terms of safety by appropriately qualified persons.

(d) Food hygiene

Food hygiene regulations already existed under the Food Act 1984, and are kept in force by the Act's transitional savings. However, these regulations are outdated and inflexible, and new controls are necessary. These new rules will take as their main objective the observance of hygienic conditions and practices in connection with the carrying out of commercial operations with respect to food and food sources.

Regulations will include requirements to ensure the good construction, maintenance, cleanliness and use of all parts of food premises and equipment and utensils used for the purposes of a food business. The disposal of refuse from food premises will be controlled as will the provision, maintenance and cleanliness of sanitary and washing facilities provided. Cleaning of equipment used for milking is also covered, with the authorised cleaning agents being specified by the Minister.

In order to clarify responsibility for these requirements under regulations, it will be possible to impose obligations of compliance on the occupier of the premises. Where the requirements relate to structural matters, the owner of the premises can also be made liable if he let the premises for purposes to which the regulations apply or allowed their use for such purposes even though the enforcement authority had made him aware of the situation. This quite clearly defines responsibilities so that one of these two persons are charged with the duty of complying with regulatory provisions.

A clause based on practicality is also provided for within Sch 1. Where the enforcement authority feels that compliance with a particular provision contained within regulations cannot be reasonably required because of the nature of the premises or the practices carried on there, it may issue a certificate of exemption. This certificate will state the requirement for which the exemption is being given, and will include any limitations and safeguards thought appropriate.

One other area may also be covered by regulations imposing requirements for the observance of hygienic conditions, and that is the provision for requiring proprietors and employees involved in a food business to undergo food hygiene training. The terms of this training would be specified within the regulations.

Section 23 gives the food authority the power to provide training courses in food hygiene for persons involved, or who intend to become involved, in a food business. These people may be proprietors or employees, and the course may be provided within the food authority's area or outside it. It is also up to the authority to decide whether or not it wishes to contribute to the expense of setting up a course, and it may contribute whether it is its expense or the expense of some other person who has decided to provide the training.

Training can be exceptionally beneficial in that it enables staff to have a better understanding of their role in the handling of food, thereby improving product quality and safety and reducing the risk of product contamination. It also improves staff standards of personal hygiene and increases efficiency.

Regulations requiring the comprehensive training of food handlers might set down the standards to be achieved by students, and might provide that all persons concerned meet those levels if they are to continue to be involved in a food business. The provisions of any requirements might allow other persons to provide courses in food hygiene training – and not just the local authority – so long as the standards set are met. This ensures that the likely demand for courses will be satisfied. Larger organisations with established training departments will already have the framework for undertaking more detailed hygiene training programmes but smaller concerns have neither the staff, time nor the resources to cope with such requirements and these will need the support of the enforcement and other agencies.

However the regulations approach this matter, their objective will be to ensure that all food handlers have a basic understanding of all the important principles of food hygiene.

(e) Labelling and describing food

Within the Act, s 15 creates an offence relating to the false description of food and to the act of misleading as to the nature of food. To supplement this control, the Minister has the power to make regulations which impose requirements or prohibitions which regulate the labelling, marking, presenting and advertising of food. The description of food is also controlled. These provisons might indicate to a person involved with such activities the type of labelling and so forth required to ensure compliance with the law as well as standardising packaging of products so that the consumer is in a better position to judge their contents. Any deviations from the content of the regulations may be classed as a false description or likely to mislead.

(f) Other regulations under s 16

The Minister is empowered to make any other regulations in addition to those mentioned above which concern food or food sources and are necessary for ensuring that the interests of public health are protected and that food complies with the food safety requirements. These additional regulations may also be for the purpose of protecting or promoting the interests of the consumer. This catch-all provision is to enable new regulations to be made in the light of technological advancement and new scientific evidence. This has the effect of keeping the legal provisions up to date whilst ensuring they remain easy to adapt without the need to invoke lengthy statute-making processes. The Minister is also able to make provision for the regulation of materials which will come into contact with food intended for human consumption. Adequately controlled food throughout the chain is of no use to the customer if it becomes contaminated because of the nature of its wrapping or contact with unsound materials.

Any regulations made in respect of contact materials may contain provisions for securing the observance of hygienic conditions and practices in connection with the carrying out of commercial operations, together with imposing requirements and prohibitions on their labelling, marking, advertising and description. Other prohibitions or regulatory provisions concerning the carrying out of commercial operations in relation to contact materials may be included as the need arises.

Within any of the regulations made under s 16 and supplemented by the provisions of Sch 1 (which may or may not be contained within the actual regulations), the power to allow for the inspection of food sources can be included. Inspection may be by an authorised officer of the enforcement authority, and would be for the purpose of seeing if the food source or any food derived from it fails to comply with those particular regulations. Where the food source or food does not comply the officer would be entitled to give notice to the person in charge of the food source that controls will be placed upon it until the time specified within the notice expires or the notice is withdrawn. These controls may take the form of preventing commercial operations from being carried out in relation to the food source and preventing its removal except to a specified place.

Completing the control of food sources is the ability to provide for the slaughter of live animals and birds which are classed as food sources, where there is present in them any substance prohibited by the regulations. Furthermore, s 16(4) provides that the Minister must have regard to restricting the use of substances which have no nutritional value as food, or as ingredients in food such as preservatives and other such additives. All regulations made must take account of this as appropriate.

Again the object of the Act is to extend enforcement by providing regulation of food safety from the initial food source to the processed food and its contact materials. An example of the regulation-making power of the Minister under s 16 and Sch 1 is the Food Hygiene (Amendment) Regulations 1990 − Temperature Control, produced in draft only a few weeks after the Act received the royal assent. These add requirements to the existing food hygiene controls which concern temperatures at which certain foods are to be kept. They are new controls for manufacturers, distributors and retail stores, and apply also to market stalls and delivery vehicles. The regulations will apply to everyone carrying on a food business: food manufacturers, processors, distributors, retailers and caterers are all covered.

Before these new provisions, temperature control was very limited in its application and was practically of very little use. Many foods were exempt from the requirements, the controls did not apply to food in the processing or preparation stage, nor to food exposed for sale and food kept available for replenishment of similar stock which was on sale. The only major controls were in respect of catering premises where food was stored for or required for serving for immediate consumption.

In the complex draft regulations set before the House of Commons by Stephen Dorrell, the junior health Minister, all foods will have to be kept at or below eight degrees Celsius. This will be enforced after 1 April 1991. Other foods most at risk of contamination with listeria monocytogenes (a bacterium which has been shown to grow at very low temperatures) will have to be kept at or below five degrees. These foods include soft cheeses, pâtés, cooked meats and other cooked produce which is usually eaten without further cooking.

Foods exempt from the regulations are chocolate and sweets, bread, biscuits and pastry, hermetically sealed and dehydrated products, ice-cream, milk or cream, uncooked meat and fish and hard cheeses. But the new controls will attempt for the first time to monitor temperature of food throughout the food chain and not just in catering establishments. From 1 April 1992, for instance, small delivery vehicles of less than seventy-five tonnes gross weight will be required to deliver foods in the controlled categories within the eight degrees limit. Larger vehicles must deliver foods within the five or eight degrees limit according to the category of the food.

In all cases, though, there will be a tolerance of two degrees of the specified temperature to allow for the defrosting cycles or for the temporary breakdown of equipment, movement of the food or a step in processing. But this will apply only for two hours. Freshly prepared food will not have to comply with the temperature requirements for limited periods of time.

According to the regulations, all food should be cooled to the required temperature without "avoidable delay". But claiming that a refrigerator is not working quickly enough will not be considered a reasonable excuse. The onus appears to be upon the client to make sure that equipment works swiftly and effectively. Any foods to be served hot must be kept above 63 degrees Celsius.

2. Regulations for enforcing Community provisions

As with the provision for the Minister to make regulations in respect of new scientific evidence and technological advancement, it is essential that any new legislation allows the integration of European Community legislation where it relates to food. The Act therefore allows the Minister to make regulations in order to fulfil any Community obligation concerning food, food sources and food contact materials and in particular the carrying out of commercial operations in relation to them (s 17(1)). Community obligation is classed as being any directive made by the European Community. Any Community directives or obligations may be integrated into United Kingdom law by the passing of regulations which secure compliance with the objective of the obligation. An example of this is the new food hygiene Community directive. This Community obligation might be implemented by regulations which would set out the objectives of the directive as regulatory provisions which must be complied with.

Directly applicable Community provisions or regulations which have been made by the European Community will be implemented by the introduction of national regulations containing provisions which direct that the contents of the European regulations are to be enforced as if made under the Act. Such national regulations could be made by the Minister, provided that the Community provision related to food, food sources or food contact materials. These national regulations might also allow for those provisions of the Act specified within them to be applicable to the Community provisions.

For example, once national regulations provide for the administration, execution and enforcement of a directly applicable Community provision, any contravention of it could mean that the requirements of the Act relating to, say, emergency control orders, would apply to the situation, provided that these orders were so specified within the national regulations.

Under s 25 the Minister can require information to be given regarding food, substances or contact materials and he may require this by order. Disclosure of any information obtained by such an order which relates to an individual business cannot be disclosed unless permission is obtained in writing from the person carrying on the business. However, where compliance with any Community obligation requires its disclosure, permission in writing does not have to be obtained.

3. Novel foods and special designations for milk

Regulatory powers exist under s 18 whereby Ministers can control novel foods (as in foods limited to, or not previously used for, human consumption) or novel food sources. This power extends to the control of imports of novel foods (s 18(1)) and to the prescription of the arrangements for the special designation of milk (s 18(2)).

The first subsection allows regulations to contain prohibitions of process such as irradiation, or prohibiting the importation of any food that has been subject to irradiation. Genetically modified food sources or food derived from such sources may also be controlled in that associated commercial operations can be prohibited. The term "genetically modified food source" is defined by s 18(4) as being the modification of genes or genetic material of a food source by artificial techniques, inheritance or replication from modified genetic material. It is possible for the Minister to provide exclusions within any regulations from the prohibitions imposed, and also to specify an authorised place of entry where prohibited imports may in fact be imported.

Milk of any description can be prescribed a designation by regulations made under s 18, including goats' milk and other less common milk. This is known as a special designation and the enforcement authority will be allowed to issue a licence allowing producers and sellers of milk to use it. Finally the regulations may also prohibit all sales of milk for human consumption unless they have a special designation or the Minister's consent. This tightening up of the controls relating to milk is welcome, particularly in that milk of all kinds is now covered and the legislation does not apply solely to cows' milk. This is an important move as goat and sheep's milk is becoming increasingly popular. Provisions made under s 18 will be complicated by the fact that legislation within Scotland is different from that in the rest of the United Kingdom. With very few exceptions all milk within Scotland must be heat treated, something which has dramatically reduced the incidence of milk-related food poisoning. The hope is that any new legislation introduced under the Act which is aimed at the review of milk legislation should include a requirement that extends the heat treatment of all milk to the rest of the United Kingdom. Not only would it provide for consistency in the legislation; it would also ensure that the public are better protected.

4. Registration and licensing of food premises

Before the Act there was no way in which premises used for food businesses could be legally identified. Identification was a haphazard affair. The Act has introduced a ministerial power to make regulations which would allow for the registration or licensing by enforcement authorities of premises used or proposed to be used for food businesses and for the prohibition of the use of premises not so registered or licensed (s 19(1)). The power to introduce a licensing scheme is qualified, however, by s 19(2) in that it is exercisable only to secure that food complies with food safety requirements, or is in the interests of public health, or for promoting the interests of the consumer.

Where regulations do provide for either a licensing or registration scheme, in order to allow for ease of administration certain transitional provisions exist which come into operation on the death of a person registered or in possession of a licence effected under those regulations. The dead person's personal representative, widow or other member of the family will have the benefit of the licence or registration for three months after his death or any longer period allowed by the enforcement authority. After this time a new application under the regulations must be made (s 43).

Although a system of registration will enable local authorities to target their enforcement action more effectively, it is seen by some as merely an administrative exercise since registration is as of right with no fee payable. An effective licensing system would, on the other hand, ensure that consumers were better protected by providing a prior approval scheme. Food businesses not operating or conforming to the conditions laid down would not be issued with a licence and would not then be allowed to continue to operate.

It does seem likely, however, that regulations requiring registration will be introduced. These will cover all commercial and permanent food premises, mobile catering vehicles, refrigerated container transport and premises used for food businesses for only a short time such as catering for sport or entertainment events. Other businesses already required to register, such as dairies and slaughterhouses, will be exempt as will charitable and social organisations with no permanent food premises of their own. This is aimed at the activities of organisations such as the Women's Institute.

5. Supplemental provisions

Regulations made under Part II of the Act can include general provisions to improve their effectiveness. They may prohibit or regulate commercial operations which fail to comply with the regulations or where an offence against the regulations has been committed (or would have been had the act or omission taken place within Great Britain). These commercial operations will have to be in relation to food, food sources or food contact materials (s 26(1)(a)).

Where, according to the regulations, food does fall within this subsection there may also be a provision included in any regulations which allows this food to be treated as not complying with the food safety requirements for the purposes of s 9 (inspection and seizure of food). In addition, the keeping of records, production of returns, the periods for which and the conditions subject to which licences may be issued, the alterations of conditions, cancellations, suspensions and revocation of licences, details as to the way in which offences may be tried, maintenance of registers, appeal matters and penalties can be included within the regulations.

All functions described within this chapter and Chapter 3 make up the detailed body of law which is now the basis of consumer protection for food safety matters. To facilitate the exercise of these functions, both those of the Act which have been formulated and those of subordinate legislation which have yet to be made, a special supplemental provision exists which allows the Minister to obtain from a food business both information and samples which are required for surveillance purposes (s 25). This would be done by order and has the effect of strengthening the Government's food surveillance programme including its extension to cover microbiological food safety.

Every person who carries on a food business of a certain specified class can be required by Ministerial order to assist authorised persons in the taking of samples and to give those persons any information required within the order. Samples may be taken of any food or substance which is sold or is intended to be sold for human consumption, any substance sold for use in the preparation of food for human consumption and any contact material which is sold and intended to come into contact with the food for such consumption. The food, substances and contact materials must be of a class specified in the order and the act of sale must be in the course of a relevant business (s 25(2)).

Disclosure of any information obtained by an order under s 25 which relates to an individual business cannot be made unless the person carrying on the business consents or the Minister directs its disclosure because it is necessary for the purposes of the Act or for any corresponding Community obligation. "For the purposes of the Act" includes for the purposes of deciding whether or not food complies with the food safety requirements, of protecting or promoting the interests of the consumer or where it is in the interests of public health. To disclose for any other reason is an offence.

6. Codes of practice

To supplement the details of any regulations the Minister has the power to issue codes of practice for the guidance of food authorities. These codes will contain recommended practice for the execution and enforcement of the Act, and will cover such areas as the frequency of inspection appropriate for different types of premises and details of inspection procedures. They will have the effect of standardising enforcement.

The food authority is required by s 40 to have regard to any relevant provisions of any code of practice and to comply with any direction given by the Minister which requires specific steps to be taken for compliance with the code. Failure of an authority to do this can mean that the matter becomes subject to a writ of *mandamus* in England and Wales and to an order of the Court of Sessions (s 45 Court of Sessions Act 1988) in Scotland. Before using the power to issue codes, the Minister must consult interested organisations and persons as to the conduct of the code, especially where their interests are likely to be substantially affected by its introduction.

7. Defences

There are three defences available under the Act: where the offence was due to the fault of another person (s 20), where due diligence was exercised (s 21), and where publication was in the course of a business (s 22).

Under s 20 the commission of an offence under the Act by one person may be due to the act of another. If this is the case, the other person can be charged and convicted of the offence whether or not the person actually committing the offence is prosecuted. The objective of the section is to mitigate the hardship which may be caused by the conviction of a person who, without guilty intention and in spite of the exercise of diligence, commits an offence under the Act. Such a provision can be used by defendants against suppliers or employers.

A new statutory defence exists under s 21. Under previous food law the defence of warranty allowed retailers to claim that all they had done was to sell food manufactured by someone else and it was that person who had committed the offence and not themselves. In the case of multiple retailers, their considerable bargaining power has been used to exert pressure on manufacturers to reduce prices which in some cases has led to a lowering of quality standards. The existence of the warranty defence has allowed them to escape any liability in law for their actions in this particular respect. In the case of importers a warranty issued from abroad has again provided an easy escape route in the event of challenge from enforcement agencies and has effectively allowed them to compete on unequal terms with British manufacturers. Multiple retailers have naturally pointed out the need for the retention of the warranty defence to avoid unnecessary prosecutions against them for, say, foreign bodies in manufactured foods which are clearly beyond their control. This argument does not, however, hold up to scrutiny because if there are no precautions which can be reasonably taken under a given set of circumstances then none need be taken. A court is unlikely to rule that multiple retailers should undertake extensive analysis in respect of foreign bodies, this is tantamount to looking for a needle in a haystack.

Such a defence has not been available for retailers who sell faulty goods which are not classed as food. Retailers selling such faulty items can be prosecuted unless they show that they made all reasonable checks to ensure that the product was safe.

The new defence makes everyone in the food chain more legally accountable for the safety of the food they sell so that they will have to be more careful about what they buy and how they store and sell it.

Section 21 gives a general defence to a person who can prove that he has taken all reasonable precautions and exercised all due diligence to avoid commission of the offence by him or any person under his control. For the main offences under ss 8, 14 and 15, special provision is made for a person who neither prepared the food himself nor imported it into Great Britain. Such a person is deemed to have exercised due diligence if he can show that the commission of the offence was due to the act of another person not under his control or due to reliance upon information provided by such a person. Also he must show that he carried out checks or reasonably relied on checks carried out by his supplier and that he did not know and had no reason to suspect at the time that his action amounted to an offence. He is also deemed to have exercised due diligence if he can show that the product was not sold under his brand name, that the offence was due to an act of a person outside his control or due to reliance on information supplied by such a person, and that he did not know and could not reasonably have been expected to know at the time of the offence that his action amounted to an offence. If the defendant alleges that the offence was due to some other person he must provide information in writing to the prosecutor concerning that person at least seven clear days before the hearing. Where he has appeared before the court before in connection with the offence, this time period is altered to within one month of his appearance. Otherwise he cannot rely on the defence.

Section 22 provides a special defence for businesses who publish an offending advertisement in good faith during the normal course of business. The person publishing must have had no reason to suspect that its publication would constitute an offence under the Act.

Whether the defendant has or has not exercised all due diligence is a question of fact to be decided by the court. However the High Court has stated that a court will interfere if there is no evidence to support a finding on this point (*R C Hammett Ltd* v *Crabb* (1931)).

Chapter 5

Administration and enforcement

In this chapter the powers of entry necessary for enforcement officers to carry out their duties under the Act are explained. Other administrative and enforcement provisions contained within Part III are then discussed, illustrating how the mechanics of legal application work. Miscellaneous matters not covered in earlier chapters are then considered, leading finally to the conclusion.

1. Powers of entry

Section 32 gives authorised officers powers of entry to premises at all reasonable hours for the purpose of ascertaining whether there has been an offence under the Act and for the purpose of enforcing its provisions. Provisions in relation to warrants are included as well as those relating to inspection, seizure and detention of records. The disclosure of information obtained when using these powers of entry is also prohibited. Although environmental health officers have always had the right to enter premises under food law, the Act provides for the first time the power for trading standards officers to enter food processing factories and carry out an inspection for matters relating to compositional and labelling law. The section does not allow entry to premises where a diseased animal or bird is kept, as determined by the Animal Health Act 1981. Only the local authority empowered by this Act may afford any entry in these circumstances.

The power to enter under this section applies to any premises within the authority's area where the purpose of entry is to determine whether there has been a contravention of provisions of the Act or its regulations. "Any premises" includes manufacturing, wholesaling and retailing premises by virtue of the definition of the word. It also applies to any business premises where the purpose of entry is to see if evidence regarding any contravention of the Act is present.

An officer can enter any premises in the authority's area to see if a contravention exists, or to enforce the Act, and can enter any business premises inside or outside the authority's area to see if evidence of a contravention exists, so long as this contravention is within their area (s 32(1)). Many businesses now operate across local authority boundaries and perhaps the head office in one area may contain evidence of food law contravention in another area. The authority in whose area the food law contravention occurred would, by s 32, have the right to enter the head office to determine if evidence existed, even though this office was outside its area.

Entry is restricted to reasonable hours, reasonable time being a question of fact. Any time during opening hours is ordinarily reasonable and special justification would be necessary for an inspector to request premises to be opened outside such hours (*Small* v *Buckley* (1875)). The authorised officer must show, if required, a duly authenticated document with authentication being as provided for by s 124 Food Act 1984. This phrase does not mean that right of entry can only be exercised if there is someone present who can require the document to be produced (*Grove* v *Eastern Gas Board* (1952)).

The right of entry also applies to premises used only as a private dwelling house, provided it is for the purposes discussed above. However, entry is not as of right unless the occupier has been given twenty-four hours' notice of the officer's intent to enter. What constitutes a satisfactory notice is a question of fact for the justices to decide.

An important point in relation to entry is that there is an implied licence for authorised officers, and in fact members of the public, to go through the gates of premises, walk to the premises and knock on the door. Only when the visitor is asked to leave is the licence revoked, and any person must be given a reasonable time to leave (*Robson* v *Hallett* (1967)).

It is clear from s 32 (2) and (3) that forcible entry requires a warrant. A warrant is obtained from a justice of the peace, who must be satisfied that there is a reasonable ground for entry in order to carry out any of those activities mentioned in s 32(1). He must also be satisfied that the officer was refused entry to the premises, or that the refusal was imminent, and that the occupier had been told that an application for a warrant was going to be made — sworn written information affirming the relevant facts will be required to satisfy the justice.

If the reason for entry would be defeated if admission were applied for, or if notice were given that a warrant will be applied for, the justice may grant a warrant provided he is satisfied that there is a reasonable ground for entry. This also applies if the case is one of urgency or the premises are unoccupied or the occupier is temporarily absent. Entry with a warrant may be by reasonable force. Whatever the nature of the entry, the authorised officer, who may take other persons with him to effect entry if he thinks it necessary, must leave unoccupied premises secure against unauthorised entry (s 32(4)).

By virtue of s 32(3), a warrant issued under s 32(2) continues in force for a period of one month; however, each warrant can be used to effect one entry only, and indeed only one search and seizure of articles (*R* v *Adams* (1980)). A second warrant must be obtained to authorise a second entry; if the same warrant is used, the entry may be classed as unlawful. However, evidence obtained as a result of an unlawful entry may be admissible in proceedings provided that its prejudicial effect does not outweigh its probative value. If it does, the judge has the discretion to refuse to admit it. The judge has no discretion to refuse admittance because of the manner in which the evidence was obtained (*R* v *Sang* (1980)).

Where entry is gained under s 32, either with or without a warrant, the authorised officer is allowed by s 32 (5) and (6) to inspect records relating to a food business and seize and detain any which may be required as evidence in any proceedings brought under the Act or its regulations. This is a new power, one which implements the provisions of the official directive on the Control of Foods. The power to seize such records also gives an implied power to take photocopies and photographs.

In the light of common office practice, provision is made for access to be gained to records kept on a computer system (s 32(5)(a) and (b); s 32(6)(b)). The officer is allowed access to the computer to inspect and check its operation in connection with the keeping of those records, and he may request any person concerned with its operation to give him any assistance he requires. Not only does this apply to the computer, but also to any associated apparatus or material used in connection with the records. He may also request that the records be assimilated in such a form from the computer that they may be taken away and used if required as evidence in proceedings.

Information obtained by way of entry to the premises about the trade secrets of a business can only be disclosed in the course of the officer's duty. Any other disclosure is an offence under s 32(7).

If an officer requests entry at a reasonable hour and in compliance with s 32 − or attempts to enter by means of a warrant obtained from a justice of the peace − a person who intentionally obstructs him is guilty of an offence (s 33). The offence is one of obstruction of an officer in the course of his duties, and relates not only to the power to enter premises but also to the obstruction of an officer or person acting in the execution of the Act as a whole. Note that the person in question must in fact act in the execution of the Act and it is not enough merely to purport to act in this way (*David* v *Lisle* (1936)). Intentional obstruction in this way, or failure to assist or give information to any person acting in the execution of the Act, is an offence if the assistance or request for information was reasonably required. The giving of false or misleading information or the reckless provision of it is also an offence.

Intentional obstruction means a deliberate act, as opposed to an accidental or inadvertent act (*R* v *Senior* (1899)), and therefore *mens rea* is essential. Consequently an employer cannot be liable for offences of a servant or employee in the course of employment unless the employer himself also committed the act or had been party to it (*Rice* v *Connolly* (1966)). Obstruction need not involve physical violence; but standing by and doing nothing (unless there is a duty to act) does not amount to an offence of obstruction.

The section relating to obstruction (s 33) does not require a person to give information or provide an answer to any question which later might incriminate him in any legal proceedings. To require otherwise would be inconsistent with the rules of natural justice. Of course all requests for information and so forth must be done in accordance with the relevant provisions of the Police and Criminal Evidence Act 1986, particularly if the subject matter obtained is necessary as evidence for proceedings. Those rules relating to contemporaneous notes, cautions, interviews and confessions must all be adhered to so as to ensure admissibility of evidence and credibility of the enforcement agency.

2. Enforcement and administration – basic provisions

The initial enforcement provisions are those contained within s 6 of the Act. This establishes by whom the various provisions are to be enforced and enables Ministers to take over particular functions of food authorities in particular cases. Within s 6(2) a duty is placed upon each food authority to enforce and execute within its area the provisions of the Act. This will ensure that local authorities target a part of their resources to food control rather than rely on existing discretionary powers.

On the question of administration, the Minister himself will decide by order which level of government will be responsible for enforcing the respective safety and consumer protection provisions (s 6(4)). In addition, s 6(4) provides that any regulations or orders made under the Act shall indicate within them which authority is to enforce them. The choice of authority ranges from the Minister, food authorities, borough, district, county and various London councils, to the Commissioners of Customs and Excise in the case of regulations. The authority named will be the enforcement authority for those provisions; it will be empowered to execute its duties under the appropriate Statutory Instrument.

3. Public analysts

Certain large authorities employ a public analyst directly, while others retain the services of private consultant analysts who may serve more than one food authority. Whatever the choice, one or more persons must be appointed to act as analyst for that local authority's area (s 27). The person appointed must have the qualifications prescribed by regulations made by the Minister, or those approved by him. If an authority appoints one public analyst only, it may appoint a suitably qualified deputy to act in his absence from office. The deputy is to be treated as the public analyst during this time, and subs(4) ensures that the provisions of s 27 relating to the analyst relate also to the deputy.

If a person is engaged directly or indirectly in any food business in any area, he cannot be appointed under s 27 to act as public analyst for that area (subs(2)). That person may be classed as being so engaged if he has made arrangements with a food business and these arrangements have been prescribed by regulations made by the Minister, and are considered to be involvement with a business.

Although the submission of a sample for analysis is not essential for proceedings under the Act, the majority of prosecutions under the relevant provisions (ss 7 – 15) will be based upon a certificate of analysis issued by a public analyst appointed under s 27. The public analyst is therefore a key figure in food law administration on whose skill and expertise a successful enforcement depends.

It is also mandatory for the authority appointing the analyst to pay him any fees or remuneration agreed. These fees may be in addition to any received by the analyst under the Act and the agreement to pay can be subject to a condition that any fees received by him are paid to the authority. The analyst does have the right to demand in advance from a person who is not an officer of the authority, but who has submitted a sample to him, payment of such fees as the authority has fixed.

Section 28 allows a food authority or a regional council in Scotland to provide facilities for microbiological examination of samples for the purposes of the Act.

4. Sampling and analysis

Under s 29, the authorised officer of an enforcement authority has the power to purchase a sample of food or any substance used in the preparation of food. In addition he can take a sample of any food or substance provided that it appears to him that it was sold or intended for sale for human consumption and that it is present on premises which he has the power to enter under s 32 of the Act.

These powers extend to samples of food sources, contact materials or any articles or substances which he has reason to believe may be required as evidence in proceedings under the Act. Such powers are wide and comprehensive but in practice are limited to samples intended for sale and sold for human consumption.

Where a sample is obtained under s 29, the authorised officer must submit it to the public analyst in the authority's area where it was procured, or in the authorised officer's authority's area, if he feels it requires analysis (s 30(1)(a)). He may also submit it for examination if he considers it necessary (s 30(1)(b)).

The discretion open to the sampling officer is to decide whether or not a sample should in fact be analysed. A sample may, for example, be examined but not analysed, and proceedings may be brought on the evidence of that examination without any analysis.

A person other than an authorised officer, being perhaps a private citizen or commercial organisation, may submit a sample to be analysed by the public analyst for the area in which the purchase was made or submit it for examination (s 30(2)).

There is no insistence on analysis since it is contemplated that satisfactory proof of the nature or composition of an article may well be given in some other way. The officer may be able to determine without analysis that an article of food sold was not of the nature demanded, for example.

An authorised officer is one who is authorised by the enforcement authority in writing. Such officers may make their purchases by deputies or agents (*Horder* v *Scott* (1880)). If this were not the case, the inspector would have to visit the shop personally in order to procure the sample and this would limit the operation of a very beneficial provision. *Tyler* v *Dairy Supply Co Ltd* (1908) is authority for the view that a sample may be taken by an agent of the officer, but how far a sampling officer may delegate his functions is a question which can hardly be regarded as settled.

Procuring samples means either taking or purchasing. *Marston* v *Wrington Vale Dairies Ltd* (1963) established the difference between the two. To take is to procure without purchase; and the person from whom the sample is taken may be reimbursed the value of the sample (*Southwell* v *Ross* (1945)). The term does not include receiving from a private purchaser food about which the purchaser subsequently complains (*Leach* v *United Dairies Ltd* (1949)).

Any food submitted for analysis under s 30 can be submitted to the public analyst in some other area if the office of the analyst in the area in question is vacant or if the analyst feels that for any reason he cannot carry out the analysis. In this last situation the analyst may determine to whom the sample should be sent, including any food examiner in the case of the examination of food.

The food analyst or examiner must analyse or examine a sample submitted to him as soon as practicable, requiring payment in advance of reasonable fees he feels are necessary. He may require these from any person other than an authorised officer of the area for which the food analyst or examiner is appointed. An analyst or examiner must give a certificate specifying the result of the analysis or examination which is signed by him although analysis or examination may be made by any person acting under his direction (s 30(7)). These certificates, documents purporting to be such certificates or copies of them, are sufficient evidence of the facts contained within them in any proceedings. Acceptability of the certificate as sufficient evidence is overruled only where the other party requires that the food analyst or examiner be called as a witness. "Food analyst" is given the meaning of a public analyst or any other suitably qualified person with the requisite qualifications. These qualifications are those prescribed in regulations made by the Minister or those approved by him. "Food examiner" means any person who possesses requisite qualifications to carry out examinations for the purposes of the Act.

By regulations the Minister may modify or supplement the provisions contained in ss 29 and 30 (s 31). Section 31(2) contains specific matters which these regulations may cover, without prejudicing the general power to modify or supplement. These specific matters include the matters relevant in determining if and when samples are to be taken, the manner of procuring samples, the method of dealing with them, to whom parts of samples are to be given, notices and information required in relation to the person in charge of the articles sampled, methods of analysis or examination and classification of the results, the circumstances which preclude food analysts or examiners from analysing or examining particular samples, and the circumstances which require the submission of samples to the Government chemist, or to any other food analyst or examiner that the Minister may direct or to any person determined by the regulations.

5. Offences

Time limits for the institution of proceedings have been extended by s 34 from the previously inadequate two months to twelve months from the date of discovery by the prosecutor of the offence. However, no prosecution for an offence under the Act can be made after the expiry of three years from the commission of the offence. This provision is useful to both industry and the enforcement agencies alike. Time is now available to overcome the practical difficulties of investigating complex issues posed by modern problems; and enough time is now allowed for a "negotiated settlement" in any dispute before resort is made to the institution of proceedings.

Section 35 sets the penalties for offences under the Act. Any person guilty of the offence of obstruction will be liable on summary conviction to a fine not exceeding £2,000 or to a term of imprisonment not in excess of three months or both (s 35(1)).

Subsections (2) and (3) set the penalties for other offences under the Act. For offences under s 7 (rendering food injurious to health), s 8 (selling food that does not comply with the food safety requirements) and s 14 (selling food not of the nature, substance or quality demanded by the purchaser) the penalty is a maximum of two years' imprisonment or an unlimited fine or both on indictment. For a summary conviction the imprisonment term is six months or a maximum £20,000 fine or both. All other offences within the Act carry the same maximum penalties on indictment, but a maximum of six months' imprisonment and/or a maximum £2,000 fine summarily.

A person convicted of an offence under the Act may lose any licence or registration he holds which enables him to keep a slaughterhouse or knacker's yard as provided for by s 1 Slaughterhouses Act (England and Wales) and, in the case of Scotland, ss 4 and 6 Slaughter of Animals (Scotland) Act 1980.

These offence provisions of the Act use the term "shall be liable". This is an absolute application in that once the offence has been committed that person is liable. Although the food authority has a duty to enforce the provisions of the Act, it does not have a duty to prosecute in every case. In *Smedleys Ltd* v *Breed* (1974), the House of Lords was critical of the local authority's bringing proceedings. The offence concerned the company supplying a tin of peas that contained a hawk moth which was almost indistinguishable from the peas. Viscount Dilhorne stated that "where it is apparent that a prosecution does not serve the interests of consumers, the justices may think fit, even if they find that the Act has been contravened, to grant an absolute discharge". Consequently, it would seem that decisions as to conviction for an offence under food law can turn on whether they are to the benefit of the consumer.

Offences by bodies corporate are dealt with in s 36. This provides that the manager, director, secretary or other similar post holder of a body corporate will be liable for prosecution where it is proved that he acted negligently or consented to or connived at the alleged offence. Not only will the body corporate be guilty of an offence but so will these individuals. "Director" is described within s 36(2) as including a member of a body corporate which has been established by an enactment for the purposes of carrying on an industry (or part of it) by national ownership. This body corporate must be one whose affairs are managed by its members.

There is authority for the view that an individual's consent presupposes knowledge (*Re Caughey, ex parte Ford* [1876] 1 Ch D 521 at page 528). Yet it is thought that actual knowledge is not necessary (*Knox* v *Boyd* (1941)).

Connivance, it has been said, implies knowledge of and acquiescence in the offence committed, but it seems that actual knowledge again is not required, with mere suspicion of the offence being sufficient. However negligence or inattention is insufficient to constitute connivance (*Rogers* v *Rogers* (1830)). The section itself does include the act of negligence as sufficient for the offence to attach to the individual. This term in the context of the Act may be thought of as implying failure to perform a duty of which the person knows or ought to know (*Re Hughes, Rea* v *Black* (1943)).

A "director, manager, secretary or other similar officers" has also been the subject of case law. In *Registrar of Restrictive Trading Agreements* v *W H Smith & Son Ltd* (1969) it was held by the Court of Appeal that a branch manager of a company is not a "manager or officer". A person is a "manager" who has involvement in the management of the whole affairs of the company. An "officer" has a similar connotation. These terms might include someone who does not manage, such as the secretary or auditor, but on the managerial side a person is not an officer unless he concerns himself with the management of the company's affairs at the centre of things, or is part of the governing body.

6. Appeals

An appeal to a magistrates' court (England and Wales) or sheriff (Scotland) is available where any person feels that the enforcement authority acted wrongly in the decision to serve an improvement notice (s 10), in the refusal to issue compliance certificates in cases where prohibition orders (s 11) and emergency prohibition notices and orders (s 12) have been served, and finally in the case where an authority refuses, cancels, suspends or revokes any licence granted by regulations made under the Act (s 37). However, in this last category, if the regulations themselves provide for an appeal to a tribunal in such instances appeal by this section will not be available – the form of appeal set by the regulations must be followed.

The procedure for appeal under s 37 is by way of complaint for an order to the magistrates' court with the Magistrates' Courts Act 1980 controlling the procedure, and by summary application to the sheriff in Scotland. The right to these appeals must be included in the original document which notifies the affected person of the decision to serve an improvement notice or do any of the other things to which the appeal provisions attach. It is also necessary to state the period within which the appeal may be brought. The right to appeal is one of rehearing by the court of the whole issue; the court is not limited to reviewing the correctness or otherwise of the grounds for an authority's decision. On appeal, therefore, the court is bound to form an opinion of its own and is entitled to substitute it for that of the authority concerned (*Stepney Borough Council* v *Joffe* (1949)).

Further appeal to the Crown Court is possible under s 38 where an aggrieved person considers it necessary because the magistrates' court or sheriff has dismissed an appeal made to it under s 37, or where a prohibition order (s 11), emergency prohibition order (s 12) or the cancellation of a licence to keep a slaughterhouse or knacker's yard (s 35) has been effected by a magistrates' court or the sheriff.

Where an appeal is made against the decision to serve an improvement notice as provided for by s 37(1)(a), the court considering the appeal may cancel, affirm or alter the notice as it thinks fit according to the circumstances. An appeal of this nature is classed as pending until it is finally disposed of, is withdrawn or is struck out for want of prosecution. But where the period for compliance stated in the notice includes a day upon which the appeal may be classed as pending then this day must be taken out of the period and the period extended to run its full course and take account of that day.

7. Instruments and documents

The various powers of the Minister(s) to make regulations and orders under the Act include the power to do certain other things by virtue of s 48. He may apply any other enactments which contain provisions similar to the content of the regulations; he may make different provisions for different cases, classes of case, areas and classes of business and provide for such exceptions, limitations and conditions as he feels necessary. It is also possible for him to make such supplementary, incidental, consequential or transitional provisions as he thinks are required.

Regulations and orders must be made by Statutory Instrument, and are therefore subject to annulment by a resolution of either House of Parliament. Before making the regulations (except those relating to enforcement of Community provisions (s 17) and those prohibiting the importation of specified food (s 18)) he must consult representatives of interested organisations where they are likely to be affected by the contents of the Statutory Instrument.

The form, authentication and service of documents authorised or required by the Act are dealt with under s 49. Those which a food authority gives, makes or issues must be in writing, as must all the notices and applications made to the authority or its officers. The form of those documents can be prescribed by regulations made by the Minister and they must be signed on behalf of the authority by the proper officer (the officer appointed for that purpose). Any officer authorised in writing by the authority may sign the documents. This authorisation must be to an officer of that authority and must cover the type of document to be signed or refer to the particular document. For purposes of practicality, a presumption exists under s 49(4) which essentially provides that where any document appears to hold the signature of an officer who is empowered by his position within the authority to sign, or who is duly authorised as mentioned above, such document will be deemed to have been issued by the food authority until the contrary is proved.

Documents required or authorised by the Act must be given or served in a particular way (s 50): by delivering to the person or, where it is an incorporated company or body, by delivering or sending in a prepaid letter addressed to the secretary or clerk at the registered or principal office. In the case of any other person, service may be by leaving it, or sending it in a prepaid letter addressed to him, at his usual or last known residence. The service on a person by using a prepaid envelope means that it is easier to prove that the envelope was sent to a particular person. The ticket provided by a post office when sending something recorded delivery is considered good evidence.

If any person wishes to give or to serve a document on an officer, he may do this by leaving it, or sending it in a prepaid letter addressed to him, at his office (s 50(1)(b)). If the name and address of the owner or occupier of any premises cannot be found after reasonable inquiry, or the premises are unoccupied and it is necessary to serve a document under the Act, it may be served by addressing it to the "owner" or "occupier" of named premises, by delivering it to some person on the premises or affixing it to a conspicuous part of the premises. Fixing the document or a copy of it will be classed as service of the document only if there is no one on the premises to whom it can be delivered.

8. Miscellaneous matters

(a) Provision of facilities for cleansing shellfish (s 24)

Due to the nature and importance attached to shellfish for human consumption, a food authority is given the power to provide tanks and other apparatus for the cleansing of shellfish. As well as the normal methods of cleansing, the term includes germicidal treatment (s 24(4)). The provision of these facilities can be either outside or inside that food authority's area, and where any other person or authority makes such items available to the public for the cleansing process, the food authority also has the power to contribute to any expenses incurred by them in doing so.

These are obviously discretionary powers and the food authority is not under an obligation to provide facilities of this nature. The section does not authorise, however, works in relation to the provision of facilities or the actual establishment of the tanks and other apparatus where the land used is below the high water mark of ordinary spring tides. This is a direct restriction on the siting of cleansing facilities for shellfish in an attempt to ensure control of public health matters.

(b) Power of the Minister to require returns (s 41)

Each food authority has a duty to provide the Minister with information, reports and returns about the exercise of those functions assigned to it under the Act. Once the Minister requires these details, the food authority is obliged to provide it in the format requested. It is submitted that this request can ask for varying degrees of detail; it provides a method by which the Minister and his agents are able to investigate food and by which the Minister and his agents are able to investigate food-related incidents, food authority involvement and application of the Act's legal provisions.

(c) Default powers (s 42)

Where the Minister is satisfied that a food authority has failed to discharge any duty imposed by the Act, he may by order empower another food authority or one of his officers to carry out that particular duty. To do this the Minister must be satisfied that the failure to discharge the duty by the food authority affects the general interests of consumers' food (s 42(1)(b)).

It may be necessary for the Minister to hold a local inquiry – under the same code of conduct as is provided for under the Local Government Act 1972 (England and Wales) and the Local Government Act 1973 (Scotland) – to establish whether the food authority had in fact failed to discharge any duty.

Either the Minister or the food authority empowered by the Minister as a substitute authority may recover any expenses reasonably incurred by them in carrying out the default powers. To pay this, the authority in default may raise the money as if the expense had been incurred directly by it, or it may borrow the sum provided it does so as authorised by the Minister and in accordance with any regulating statutory provisions. To penalise the food authority in default by not affording it this facility to raise the money would be merely to penalise the electorate within the district who, as consumers, are among the persons whom the Act is attempting to protect.

(d) Statutory protection of officers who act in good faith (s 44)

This section provides that an officer of a food authority should not be held personally liable for his actions provided that he acted in good faith. The protection afforded by this section is necessary in view of the wide powers conferred on officers and their potential effect on business.

Provided that an officer, including an analyst of a food authority, acted in the execution of the Act, or in the belief that his actions were in execution of it — and he acted also within the scope of his employment — he will not be personally liable so long as he honestly thought that the Act required him to take those actions. It is also possible for an authority to indemnify an officer against any damages he may be liable to pay as a result of an action which was outside his scope of employment but in execution of the Act. This will only be done where the officer honestly believed that the act done was in the scope of his employ. Of course contractual law relating to employment will be important here, especially in relation to what constitutes the "scope of employment".

This does not mean that the principles of vicarious liability no longer apply. Section 44(2) specifically provides that any food authority will remain vicariously liable for the acts of its officers, so that some redress for an aggrieved party is assured.

(e) Financial provisions (ss 45 – 47)

In the execution of the Act, enforcement authorities may find it necessary to make certain charges. To enable them to impose these levies some form of legal power must be available. The Act approaches this by allowing Ministers to make regulations under s 45.

These regulations will either require charges to be made in relation to acts done by the enforcement authority when carrying out its duties under the Act, or will merely provide the authorisation for the authority to charge should it so wish. This will allow charges to be made for registration or licensing even though it remains under the control of the Minister. The extent of these charges is limited by s 45(3) and (4). Any regulations made can contain the provision that the charge be at the authority's discretion and may include a maximum and a minimum level. Where parameters for charges are set, prescribed cases can be allocated precise levels of charges and methods as to calculating the actual charges.

It is possible under s 46 for a food authority to defray expenses incurred by an officer when taking samples and having them analysed. County councils may at the discretion of the Secretary of State charge expenses incurred in the enforcement of the Act or any regulations or orders under it and may class them as expenses for special county purposes. They may also be charged as specified in the direction.

Provision is also made for remuneration of tribunal chairmen in the event of expenses arising out of hearings concerning compensation for depreciation in the value of seized food (s 9), or loss as a result of a prohibition placed upon any business or proprietor (s 12). The money is to be provided by Parliament and the appropriate allowance is to be determined by the Ministers with the approval of the Treasury (s 47).

9. Conclusion

Some aspects of current food law, although historical in origin, have remained relevant. But in the main, United Kingdom food law had failed to keep pace with the developments in food technology and research, methods of food production, retailing and merchandising and with the consumers' preference for pre-packed food, convenience food and food that keeps for a long time. Food law reform had to address both the perceived need to strengthen legal protection for the consumer and the need for an enabling framework to ensure that future developments could be provided for. The Food Act 1984 took on board the majority of the measures necessary to introduce this reform. It reflected the concern over the past few years about food standards and recognised environmental health and trading standards officers as the front line in consumer protection.

The main provisions of the new Act revise existing offences and introduce an umbrella offence of supplying food which does not comply with the food safety requirements. Powers of enforcement officers are extended in food factories and allow for speedier detention and seizure of food judged to be unsafe.

Food problems deemed to be "potentially serious" by Ministers can be dealt with by emergency control orders covering food production, importation and distribution where an imminent risk to health is found. This provision comes into force immediately. So-called novel foods and new technological developments in the food industry can be dealt with in detailed legislation adapting the new Act.

More quickly than before, local authority officers will have the power to issue improvement notices and to close down premises where there is a risk to health.

The Act does leave unsaid, however, how food safety responsibilities should be divided within local authorities. The 1984 Act divided work between counties and districts or combined it within metropolitan councils, consequently splitting duties between county trading standards officers and the district environmental health officers.

The opportunity has not been taken to deal with the problems associated with the division of responsibilities for enforcement. This division creates confusion in the public mind, is neither efficient nor productive, and does not provide a proper service to the consumer. The fact that on occasions two enforcement agencies may visit the premises is confusing, and duplication of effort is financially wasteful.

Within the London boroughs and in Scotland the district councils have all the responsibilities and functions within this sphere and the position is much clearer and more effective.

On both the trading standards side and that of the environmental health officer there is a definite lack of funding and qualified staff to enforce the legislation. Not only will it be necessary to maintain the extra £30m earmarked for authorities, but extra training of officers will be required together with a suitably fair system for the division of any resources between the various local authorities.

Enforcement of food law within the United Kingdom must change, perhaps even further than the Act envisages. Environmental health officers and their trading standards counterparts have a wide range of duties and responsibilities, and food law does not always have top priority.

The establishment of a single food regulation agency would ensure adequate control over, and safeguarding of, food safety. It would have regard to all matters relating to food and the protection and enhancement of public health. Food safety and hygiene would not be looked at in isolation but in association with nutrition, diet and consumer education, which are essential components towards achieving the ultimate goal of protecting and enhancing the health of the consumer.

The next battle for food safety officers in local government will come during consultations on the Act's regulations when the food industry lobby may press for looser interpretation and enforcement. The introduction of a general safety requirement would have assisted the enforcement agencies in their attempts to improve food safety attitudes. The Act does not include a general safety requirement for food such as the one for suppliers of other consumer goods. Under the Consumer Protection Act 1986 a general safety requirement is implemented. Essentially this provides that a person is guilty of an offence if he supplies consumer goods which are not reasonably safe having regard to all the circumstances. These circumstances include the manner in which, and the purposes for which, goods are marketed, the get-up of the goods, the use of any marks in relation to the goods and any instructions or warnings given with respect to the keeping, use or consumption of the goods. Standards of safety which apply to the goods in question and any reasonable means by which the goods have been made safer, taking into account the cost, likelihood and extent of any improvements, must also be considered.

The introduction of a similar requirement within the food industry would ensure that producers had a greater responsibility for the general safety of their products, including packaging and contaminants. The provision of a "general duty" would improve food safety all the way along the food chain, from safer farming methods to cooking instructions on ready-made meals.

On their own the changes made to the law by the Act, whilst providing some long-awaited improvements, will not resolve some of the fundamental problems affecting the food industry. Perhaps even more change is necessary.

Appendix

Food Safety Act 1990

PART I
Preliminary

1. – (1) In this Act "food" includes –

    (a)   drink;

    (b)   articles and substances of no nutritional value which are used for human consumption;

    (c)   chewing gum and other products of a like nature and use; and

    (d)   articles and substances used as ingredients in the preparation of food or anything falling within this subsection.

(2) In this Act "food" does not include –

    (a)   live animals or birds, or live fish which are not used for human consumption while they are alive;

    (b)   fodder or feeding stuffs for animals, birds or fish;

    (c)   controlled drugs within the meaning of the Misuse of Drugs Act 1971; or

    (d)   subject to such exceptions as may be specified in an order made by the Ministers –

        (i)   medicinal products within the meaning of the Medicines Act 1968 in respect of which product licences within the meaning of that Act are for the time being in force; or

        (ii)   other articles or substances in respect of which such licences are for the time being in force in pursuance of orders under section 104 or 105 of that Act (application of Act to other articles and substances).

(3) In this Act, unless the context otherwise requires –

"business" includes the undertaking of a canteen, club, school, hospital or institution, whether carried on for profit or not, and any undertaking or activity carried on by a public or local authority;

"commercial operation", in relation to any food or contact material, means any of the following, namely –

    (a)   selling, possessing for sale and offering, exposing or advertising for sale;

    (b)   consigning, delivering or serving by way of sale;

    (c)   preparing for sale or presenting, labelling or wrapping for the purpose of sale;

    (d)   storing or transporting for the purpose of sale;

    (e)   importing and exporting;

and, in relation to any food source, means deriving food from it for the purpose of sale or for purposes connected with sale;

"contact material" means any article or substance which is intended to come into contact with food;

"food business" means any business in the course of which commercial operations with respect to food or food sources are carried out;

"food premises" means any premises used for the purpose of a food business;

"food source" means any growing crop or live animal, bird or fish from which food is intended to be derived (whether by harvesting, slaughtering, milking, collecting eggs or otherwise);

"premises" includes any place, any vehicle, stall or moveable structure and, for such purposes as may be specified in an order made by the Ministers, any ship or aircraft of a description so specified.

(4) The reference in subsection (3) above to preparing for sale shall be construed, in relation to any contact material, as a reference to manufacturing or producing for the purpose of sale.

2. – (1) For the purposes of this Act –

    (a)   the supply of food, otherwise than on sale, in the course of a business; and

    (b)   any other thing which is done with respect to food and is specified in an order made by the Ministers,

shall be deemed to be a sale of the food, and references to purchasers and purchasing shall be construed accordingly.

(2) This Act shall apply –

    (a)   in relation to any food which is offered as a prize or reward or given away in connection with any entertainment to which the public are admitted, whether on payment of money or not, as if the food were, or had been, exposed for sale by each person concerned in the organisation of the entertainment;

    (b)   in relation to any food which, for the purpose of advertisement or in furtherance of any trade or business, is offered as a prize or reward or given away, as if the food were, or had been, exposed for sale by the person offering or giving away the food; and

    (c)   in relation to any food which is exposed or deposited in any premises for the purpose of being so offered or given away as mentioned in paragraph (a) or (b) above, as if the food were, or had been, exposed for sale by the occupier of the premises;

and in this subsection "entertainment" includes any social gathering, amusement, exhibition, performance, game, sport or trial of skill.

3. – (1) The following provisions shall apply for the purposes of this Act.

(2) Any food commonly used for human consumption shall, if sold or offered, exposed or kept for sale, be presumed, until the contrary is proved, to have been sold or, as the case may be, to have been or to be intended for sale for human consumption.

(3) The following, namely –

(a) any food commonly used for human consumption which is found on premises used for the preparation, storage, or sale of that food; and

(b) any article or substance commonly used in the manufacture of food for human consumption which is found on premises used for the preparation, storage or sale of that food,

shall be presumed, until the contrary is proved, to be intended for sale, or for manufacturing food for sale, for human consumption.

(4) Any article or substance capable of being used in the composition or preparation of any food commonly used for human consumption which is found on premises on which that food is prepared shall, until the contrary is proved, be presumed to be intended for such use.

4. – (1) In this Act –

"the Minister" means, subject to subsection (2) below –

(a) in relation to England and Wales, the Minister of Agriculture, Fisheries and Food or the Secretary of State;

(b) in relation to Scotland, the Secretary of State;

"the Ministers" means –

(a) in relation to England and Wales, the following Ministers acting jointly, namely, the Minister of Agriculture, Fisheries and Food and the Secretaries of State respectively concerned with health in England and food and health in Wales;

(b) in relation to Scotland, the Secretary of State.

(2) In this Act, in its application to emergency control orders, "the Minister" means the Minister of Agriculture, Fisheries and Food, or the Secretary of State.

5. – (1) Subject to subsections (3) and (4) below, the food authorities in England and Wales are –

(a) as respects each London borough, district or non-metropolitan county, the council of that borough, district or county;

(b) as respects the City of London (including the Temples), the Common Council;

(c) as respects the Inner Temple or the Middle Temple, the appropriate Treasurer.

(2) Subject to subsection (3)(a) below, the food authorities in Scotland are the islands or district councils.

(3) Where any functions under this Act are assigned –

(a) by an order under section 2 or 7 of the Public Health (Control of Disease) Act 1984, to a port health authority or, by an order under section 172 of the Public Health (Scotland) Act 1897, to a port local authority;

(b) by an order under section 6 of the Public Health Act 1936, to a joint board for a united district; or

(c) by an order under paragraph 15(6) of Schedule 8 to the Local Government Act 1985, to a single authority for a metropolitan county,

any reference in this Act to a food authority shall be construed, so far as relating to those functions, as a reference to the authority to whom they are so assigned.

(4) The Ministers may by order provide, either generally or in relation to cases of a particular description, that any functions under this Act which are exercisable concurrently –

    (a)   as respects a non-metropolitan district, by the council of that district and the council of the non-metropolitan county;

    (b)   as respects the Inner Temple or the Middle Temple, by the appropriate Treasurer and the Common Council,

shall be exercisable solely by such one of those authorities as may be specified in the order.

(5) In this section –

"the appropriate Treasurer" means the Sub-Treasurer in relation to the Inner Temple and the Under Treasurer in relation to the Middle Temple;

"the Common Council" means the Common Council of the City of London;

"port local authority" includes a joint port local authority.

(6) In this Act "authorised officer", in relation to a food authority, means any person (whether or not an officer of the authority) who is authorised by them in writing, either generally or specially, to act in matters arising under this Act; but if regulations made by the Ministers so provide, no person shall be so authorised unless he has such qualifications as may be prescribed by the regulations.

6. – (1) In this Act "the enforcement authority", in relation to any provisions of this Act or any regulations or orders made under it, means the authority by whom they are to be enforced and executed.

(2) Every food authority shall enforce and execute within their area the provisions of this Act with respect to which the duty is not imposed expressly or by necessary implication on some other authority.

(3) The Ministers may direct, in relation to cases of a particular description, or a particular case, that any duty imposed on food authorities by subsection (2) above shall be discharged by the Ministers or the Minister and not by those authorities.

(4) Regulations or orders under this Act shall specify which of the following authorities are to enforce and execute them, either generally or in relation to cases of a particular description or a particular area, namely –

    (a)   the Ministers, the Minister, food authorities and such other authorities as are mentioned in section 5(3) above; and

    (b)   in the case of regulations, the Commissioners of Customs and Excise;

and any such regulations or orders may provide for the giving of assistance and information, by any authority concerned in the administration of the regulations or orders, or of any provisions of this Act, to any other authority so concerned, for the purposes of their respective duties under them.

(5) An enforcement authority in England and Wales may institute proceedings under any provisions of this Act or any regulations or orders made under it and, in the case of the Ministers or the Minister, may take over the conduct of any such proceedings which have been instituted by some other person.

PART II
Main Provisions

Food Safety

7. – (1) Any person who renders any food injurious to health by means of any of the following operations, namely –

(a)   adding any article or substance to the food;

(b)   using any article or substance as an ingredient in the preparation of the food;

(c)   abstracting any constituent from the food; and

(d)   subjecting the food to any other process or treatment,

with intent that it shall be sold for human consumption, shall be guilty of an offence.

(2) In determining for the purposes of this section and section 8(2) below whether any food is injurious to health, regard shall be had –

(a)   not only to the probable effect of that food on the health of a person consuming it; but

(b)   also to the probable cumulative effect of food of substantially the same composition on the health of a person consuming it in ordinary quantities.

(3) In this Part "injury", in relation to health, includes any impairment, whether permanent or temporary, and "injurious to health" shall be construed accordingly.

8. – (1) Any person who –

(a)   sells for human consumption, or offers, exposes or advertises for sale for such consumption, or has in his possession for the purpose of such sale or of preparation for such sale; or

(b)   deposits with, or consigns to, any other person for the purpose of such sale or of preparation for such sale,

any food which fails to comply with food safety requirements shall be guilty of an offence.

(2) For the purposes of this Part food fails to comply with food safety requirements if –

(a)   it has been rendered injurious to health by means of any of the operations mentioned in section 7(1) above;

(b)   it is unfit for human consumption; or

(c)   it is so contaminated (whether by extraneous matter or otherwise) that it would not be reasonable to expect it to be used for human consumption in that state;

and references to such requirements or to food complying with such requirements shall be construed accordingly.

(3) Where any food which fails to comply with food safety requirements is part of a batch, lot or consignment of food of the same class or description, it shall be presumed for the purpose of this section and section 9 below, until the contrary is proved, that all of the food in that batch, lot or consignment fails to comply with those requirements.

(4) For the purposes of this Part, any part of, or product derived wholly or partly from, an animal –

(a) which has been slaughtered in a knacker's yard, or of which the carcase has been brought into a knacker's yard; or

(b) in Scotland, which has been slaughtered otherwise than in a slaughterhouse,

shall be deemed to be unfit for human consumption.

(5) In subsection (4) above, in its application to Scotland, "animal" means any description of cattle, sheep, goat, swine, horse, ass or mule; and paragraph (b) of that subsection shall not apply where accident, illness or emergency affecting the animal in question required it to be slaughtered as mentioned in that paragraph.

9. – (1) An authorised officer of a food authority may at all reasonable times inspect any food intended for human consumption which –

(a) has been sold or is offered or exposed for sale; or

(b) is in the possession of, or has been deposited with or consigned to, any person for the purpose of sale or of preparation for sale;

and subsections (3) to (9) below shall apply where, on such an inspection, it appears to the authorised officer that any food fails to comply with food safety requirements.

(2) The following provisions shall also apply where, otherwise than on such an inspection, it appears to an authorised officer of a food authority that any food is likely to cause food poisoning or any disease communicable to human beings.

(3) The authorised officer may either –

(a) give notice to the person in charge of the food that, until the notice is withdrawn, the food or any specified portion of it –

(i) is not to be used for human consumption; and

(ii) either is not to be removed or is not to be removed except to some place specified in the notice; or

(b) seize the food and remove it in order to have it dealt with by a justice of the peace;

and any person who knowingly contravenes the requirements of a notice under paragraph (a) above shall be guilty of an offence.

(4) Where the authorised officer exercises the powers conferred by subsection (3)(a) above, he shall, as soon as is reasonably practicable and in any event within 21 days, determine whether or not he is satisfied that the food complies with food safety requirements and –

(a) if he is so satisfied, shall forthwith withdraw the notice;

(b) if he is not so satisfied, shall seize the food and remove it in order to have it dealt with by a justice of the peace.

(5) Where an authorised officer exercises the powers conferred by subsection (3)(b) or (4)(b) above, he shall inform the person in charge of the food of his intention to have it dealt with by a justice of the peace and –

(a) any person who under section 7 or 8 above might be liable to a prosecution in respect of the food shall, if he attends before the justice of the peace by whom the food falls to be dealt with, be entitled to be heard and to call witnesses; and

(b)   that justice of the peace may, but need not, be a member of the court before which any person is charged with an offence under that section in relation to that food.

(6) If it appears to a justice of the peace, on the basis of such evidence as he considers appropriate in the circumstances, that any food falling to be dealt with by him under this section fails to comply with food safety requirements, he shall condemn the food and order –

(a)   the food to be destroyed or to be so disposed of as to prevent it from being used for human consumption; and

(b)   any expenses reasonably incurred in connection with the destruction or disposal to be defrayed by the owner of the food.

(7) If a notice under subsection (3)(a) above is withdrawn, or the justice of the peace by whom any food falls to be dealt with under this section refuses to condemn it, the food authority shall compensate the owner of the food for any depreciation in its value resulting from the action taken by the authorised officer.

(8) Any disputed question as to the right to or the amount of any compensation payable under subsection (7) above shall be determined by arbitration.

(9) In the application of this section to Scotland –

(a)   any reference to a justice of the peace includes a reference to the sheriff and to a magistrate;

(b)   paragraph (b) of subsection (5) above shall not apply;

(c)   any order made under subsection (6) above shall be sufficient evidence in any proceedings under this Act of the failure of the food in question to comply with food safety requirements; and

(d)   the reference in subsection (8) above to determination by arbitration shall be construed as a reference to determination by a single arbiter appointed, failing agreement between the parties, by the sheriff.

10. – (1) If an authorised officer of an enforcement authority has reasonable grounds for believing that the proprietor of a food business is failing to comply with any regulations to which this section applies, he may, by a notice served on that proprietor (in this Act referred to as an "improvement notice") –

(a)   state the officer's grounds for believing that the proprietor is failing to comply with the regulations;

(b)   specify the matters which constitute the proprietor's failure so to comply;

(c)   specify the measures which, in the officer's opinion, the proprietor must take in order to secure compliance; and

(d)   require the proprietor to take those measures, or measures which are at least equivalent to them, within such period (not being less than 14 days) as may be specified in the notice.

(2) Any person who fails to comply with an improvement notice shall be guilty of an offence.

(3) This section and section 11 below apply to any regulations under this Part which make provision –

(a)   for requiring, prohibiting or regulating the use of any process or treatment in the preparation of food; or

(b)   for securing the observance of hygienic conditions and practices in connection with the carrying out of commercial operations with respect to food or food sources.

11. – (1) If –

(a) the proprietor of a food business is convicted of an offence under any regulations to which this section applies; and

(b) the court by or before which he is so convicted is satisfied that the health risk condition is fulfilled with respect to that business,

the court shall by an order impose the appropriate prohibition.

(2) The health risk condition is fulfilled with respect to any food business if any of the following involves risk of injury to health, namely –

(a) the use for the purposes of the business of any process or treatment;

(b) the construction of any premises used for the purposes of the business, or the use for those purposes of any equipment; and

(c) the state or condition of any premises or equipment used for the purposes of the business.

(3) The appropriate prohibition is –

(a) in a case falling within paragraph (a) of subsection (2) above, a prohibition on the use of the process or treatment for the purposes of the business;

(b) in a case falling within paragraph (b) of that subsection, a prohibition on the use of the premises or equipment for the purposes of the business or any other food business of the same class or description;

(c) in a case falling within paragraph (c) of that subsection, a prohibition on the use of the premises or equipment for the purposes of any food business.

(4) If –

(a) the proprietor of a food business is convicted of an offence under any regulations to which this section applies by virtue of section 10(3)(b) above; and

(b) the court by or before which he is so convicted thinks it proper to do so in all the circumstances of the case,

the court may, by an order, impose a prohibition on the proprietor participating in the management of any food business, or any food business of a class or description specified in the order.

(5) As soon as practicable after the making of an order under subsection (1) or (4) above (in this Act referred to as a "prohibition order"), the enforcement authority shall –

(a) serve a copy of the order on the proprietor of the business; and

(b) in the case of an order under subsection (1) above, affix a copy of the order in a conspicuous position on such premises used for the purposes of the business as they consider appropriate;

and any person who knowingly contravenes such an order shall be guilty of an offence.

(6) A prohibition order shall cease to have effect –

(a) in the case of an order under subsection (1) above, on the issue by the enforcement authority of a certificate to the effect that they are satisfied that the proprietor has taken sufficient measures to secure that the health risk condition is no longer fulfilled with respect to the business;

(b) in the case of an order under subsection (4) above, on the giving by the court of a direction to that effect.

(7) The enforcement authority shall issue a certificate under paragraph (a) of subsection (6) above within three days of their being satisfied as mentioned in that paragraph; and on an application by the proprietor for such a certificate, the authority shall –

(a) determine, as soon as is reasonably practicable and in any event within 14 days, whether or not they are so satisfied; and

(b) if they determine that they are not so satisfied, give notice to the proprietor of the reasons for that determination.

(8) The court shall give a direction under subsection (6)(b) above if, on an application by the proprietor, the court thinks it proper to do so having regard to all the circumstances of the case, including in particular the conduct of the proprietor since the making of the order; but no such application shall be entertained if it is made –

(a) within six months after the making of the prohibition order; or

(b) within three months after the making by the proprietor of a previous application for such a direction.

(9) Where a magistrates' court or, in Scotland, the sheriff makes an order under section 12(2) below with respect to any food business, subsection (1) above shall apply as if the proprietor of the business had been convicted by the court or sheriff of an offence under regulations to which this section applies.

(10) Subsection (4) above shall apply in relation to a manager of a food business as it applies in relation to the proprietor of such a business; and any reference in subsection (5) or (8) above to the proprietor of the business, or to the proprietor, shall be construed accordingly.

(11) In subsection (10) above "manager", in relation to a food business, means any person who is entrusted by the proprietor with the day to day running of the business, or any part of the business.

12. – (1) If an authorised officer of an enforcement authority is satisfied that the health risk condition is fulfilled with respect to any food business, he may, by a notice served on the proprietor of the business (in this Act referred to as an "emergency prohibition notice"), impose the appropriate prohibition.

(2) If a magistrates' court or, in Scotland, the sheriff is satisfied, on the application of such an officer, that the health risk condition is fulfilled with respect to any food business, the court or sheriff shall, by an order (in this Act referred to as an "emergency prohibition order"), impose the appropriate prohibition.

(3) Such an officer shall not apply for an emergency prohibition order unless, at least one day before the date of the application, he has served notice on the proprietor of the business of his intention to apply for the order.

(4) Subsections (2) and (3) of section 11 above shall apply for the purposes of this section as they apply for the purposes of that section, but as if the reference in subsection (2) to risk of injury to health were a reference to imminent risk of such injury.

(5) As soon as practicable after the service of an emergency prohibition notice, the enforcement authority shall affix a copy of the notice in a conspicuous position on

such premises used for the purposes of the business as they consider appropriate; and any person who knowingly contravenes such a notice shall be guilty of an offence.

(6) As soon as practicable after the making of an emergency prohibition order, the enforcement authority shall –

    (a)   serve a copy of the order on the proprietor of the business; and

    (b)   affix a copy of the order in a conspicuous position on such premises used for the purposes of that business as they consider appropriate;

and any person who knowingly contravenes such an order shall be guilty of an offence.

(7) An emergency prohibition notice shall cease to have effect –

    (a)   if no application for an emergency prohibition order is made within the period of three days beginning with the service of the notice, at the end of that period;

    (b)   if such an application is so made, on the determination or abandonment of the application.

(8) An emergency prohibition notice or emergency prohibition order shall cease to have effect on the issue by the enforcement authority of a certificate to the effect that they are satisfied that the proprietor has taken sufficient measures to secure that the health risk condition is no longer fulfilled with respect to the business.

(9) The enforcement authority shall issue a certificate under subsection (8) above within three days of their being satisfied as mentioned in that subsection; and on an application by the proprietor for such a certificate, the authority shall –

    (a)   determine, as soon as is reasonably practicable and in any event within 14 days, whether or not they are so satisfied; and

    (b)   if they determine that they are not so satisfied, give notice to the proprietor of the reasons for that determination.

(10) Where an emergency prohibition notice is served on the proprietor of a business, the enforcement authority shall compensate him in respect of any loss suffered by reason of his complying with the notice unless –

    (a)   an application for an emergency prohibition order is made within the period of three days beginning with the service of the notice; and

    (b)   the court declares itself satisfied, on the hearing of the application, that the health risk condition was fulfilled with respect to the business at the time when the notice was served;

and any disputed question as to the right to or the amount of any compensation payable under this subsection shall be determined by arbitration or, in Scotland, by a single arbiter appointed, failing agreement between the parties, by the sheriff.

13. – (1) If it appears to the Minister that the carrying out of commercial operations with respect to food, food sources or contact materials of any class or description involves or may involve imminent risk of injury to health, he may, by an order (in this Act referred to as an "emergency control order"), prohibit the carrying out of such operations with respect to food, food sources or contact materials of that class or description.

(2) Any person who knowingly contravenes an emergency control order shall be guilty of an offence.

(3) The Minister may consent, either unconditionally or subject to any condition that he considers appropriate, to the doing in a particular case of anything prohibited by an emergency control order.

(4) It shall be a defence for a person charged with an offence under subsection (2) above to show –

   (a) that consent had been given under subsection (3) above to the contravention of the emergency control order; and

   (b) that any condition subject to which that consent was given was complied with.

(5) The Minister –

   (a) may give such directions as appear to him to be necessary or expedient for the purpose of preventing the carrying out of commercial operations with respect to any food, food sources or contact materials which he believes, on reasonable grounds, to be food, food sources or contact materials to which an emergency control order applies; and

   (b) may do anything which appears to him to be necessary or expedient for that purpose.

(6) Any person who fails to comply with a direction under this section shall be guilty of an offence.

(7) If the Minister does anything by virtue of this section in consequence of any person failing to comply with an emergency control order or a direction under this section, the Minister may recover from that person any expenses reasonably incurred by him under this section.

Consumer protection

14. – (1) Any person who sells to the purchaser's prejudice any food which is not of the nature or substance or quality demanded by the purchaser shall be guilty of an offence.

(2) In subsection (1) above the reference to sale shall be construed as a reference to sale for human consumption; and in proceedings under that subsection it shall not be a defence that the purchaser was not prejudiced because he bought for analysis or examination.

15. – (1) Any person who gives with any food sold by him, or displays with any food offered or exposed by him for sale or in his possession for the purpose of sale, a label, whether or not attached to or printed on the wrapper or container, which –

   (a) falsely describes the food; or

   (b) is likely to mislead as to the nature or substance or quality of any food,

shall be guilty of an offence.

(2) Any person who publishes, or is a party to the publication of, an advertisement (not being such a label given or displayed by him as mentioned in subsection (1) above which –

   (a) falsely describes any food; or

   (b) is likely to mislead as to the nature or substance or quality of any food,

shall be guilty of an offence.

(3) Any person who sells, or offers or exposes for sale, or has in his possession for the purpose of sale, any food the presentation of which is likely to mislead as to the nature or substance or quality of the food shall be guilty of an offence.

(4) In proceedings for an offence under subsections (1) or (2) above, the fact that a label or advertisement in respect of which the offence is alleged to have been committed contained an accurate statement of the composition of the food shall not preclude the court from finding that the offence was committed.

(5) In this section references to sale shall be construed as references to sale for human consumption.

Regulations

16. – (1) The Ministers may by regulations make –

(a) provision for requiring, prohibiting or regulating the presence in food or food sources of any specified substance, or any substance of any specified class, and generally for regulating the composition of food;

(b) provision for securing that food is fit for human consumption and meets such microbiological standards (whether going to the fitness of the food or otherwise) as may be specified by or under the regulations;

(c) provision for requiring, prohibiting or regulating the use of any process or treatment in the preparation of food;

(d) provision for securing the observance of hygienic conditions and practices in connection with the carrying out of commercial operations with respect to food or food sources;

(e) provision for imposing requirements or prohibitions as to, or otherwise regulating, the labelling, marking, presenting or advertising of food, and the descriptions which may be applied to food; and

(f) such other provision with respect to food or food sources, including in particular provision for prohibiting or regulating the carrying out of commercial operations with respect to food or food sources, as appears to them to be necessary or expedient –

   (i) for the purpose of securing that food complies with food safety requirements or in the interests of the public health; or

   (ii) for the purpose of protecting or promoting the interests of consumers.

(2) The Ministers may also by regulations make provision –

(a) for securing the observance of hygienic conditions and practices in connection with the carrying out of commercial operations with respect to contact materials which are intended to come into contact with food intended for human consumption;

(b) for imposing requirements or prohibitions as to, or otherwise regulating, the labelling, marking or advertising of such materials, and the descriptions which may be applied to them; and

(c) otherwise for prohibiting or regulating the carrying out of commercial operations with respect to such materials.

(3) Without prejudice to the generality of subsection (1) above, regulations under that subsection may make any such provision as is mentioned in Schedule 1 to this Act.

(4) In making regulations under subsection (1) above, the Ministers shall have regard to the desirability of restricting, so far as practicable, the use of substances of no nutritional value as foods or as ingredients of foods.

(5) In subsection (1) above and Schedule 1 to this Act, unless the context otherwise requires –

(a)   references to food shall be construed as references to food intended for sale for human consumption; and

(b)   references to food sources shall be construed as references to food sources from which such food is intended to be derived.

17. – (1) The Ministers may by regulations make such provision with respect to food, food sources or contact materials, including in particular provision for prohibiting or regulating the carrying out of commercial operations with respect to food, food sources or contact materials, as appears to them to be called for by any Community obligation.

(2) As respects any directly applicable Community provision which relates to food, food sources or contact materials and for which, in their opinion, it is appropriate to provide under this Act, the Ministers may by regulations –

(a)   make such provision as they consider necessary or expedient for the purpose of securing that the Community provision is administered, executed and enforced under this Act; and

(b)   apply such of the provisions of this Act as may be specified in the regulations in relation to the Community provision with such modifications, if any, as may be so specified.

(3) In subsections (1) and (2) above references to food or food sources shall be construed in accordance with section 16(5) above.

18. – (1) The Ministers may by regulations make provision –

(a)   for prohibiting the carrying out of commercial operations with respect to novel foods, or food sources from which such foods are intended to be derived, of any class specified in the regulations;

(b)   for prohibiting the carrying out of such operations with respect to genetically modified food sources, or foods derived from such food sources, of any class so specified; or

(c)   for prohibiting the importation of any food of a class so specified,

and (in each case) for excluding from the prohibition any food or food source which is of a description specified by or under the regulations and, in the case of a prohibition on importation, is imported at an authorised place of entry.

(2) The Ministers may also by regulations –

(a)   prescribe, in relation to milk of any description, such a designation (in this subsection referred to as a "special designation") as the Ministers consider appropriate;

(b)   provide for the issue by enforcement authorities of licences to producers and sellers of milk authorising the use of a special designation; and

(c)   prohibit, without the use of a special designation, all sales of milk for human consumption, other than sales made with the Minister's consent.

(3) In this section –

"authorised place of entry" means any port, aerodrome or other place of entry authorised by or under the regulations and, in relation to food in a particular consignment, includes any place of entry so authorised for the importation of that consignment;

"description", in relation to food, includes any description of its origin or of the manner in which it is packed;

"novel food" means any food which has not previously been used for human consumption in Great Britain, or has been so used only to a very limited extent.

(4) For the purposes of this section a food source is genetically modified if any of the genes or other genetic material in the food source –

(a) has been modified by means of an artificial technique; or

(b) is inherited or otherwise derived, through any number of replications, from genetic material which was so modified;

and in this subsection "artificial technique" does not include any technique which involves no more than, or no more than the assistance of, naturally occurring processes of reproduction (including selective breeding techniques or *in vitro* fertilisation).

19. – (1) The Ministers may by regulations make provision –

(a) for the registration by enforcement authorities of premises used or proposed to be used for the purposes of a food business, and for prohibiting the use for those purposes of any premises, which are not registered in accordance with the regulations; or

(b) subject to subsection (2) below, for the issue by such authorities of licences in respect of the use of premises for the purposes of a food business, and for prohibiting the use for those purposes of any premises except in accordance with a licence issued under the regulations.

(2) The Ministers shall exercise the power conferred by subsection (1)(b) above only where it appears to them to be necessary or expedient to do so –

(a) for the purpose of securing that food complies with food safety requirements or in the interests of the public health; or

(b) for the purpose of protecting or promoting the interests of consumers.

Defences etc

20. – Where the commission by any person of an offence under any of the preceding provisions of this Part is due to an act or default of some other person, that other person shall be guilty of the offence by virtue of this section whether or not proceedings are taken against the first-mentioned person.

21. – (1) In any proceedings for an offence under any of the preceding provisions of this Part (in this section referred to as "the relevant provision"), it shall, subject to subsection (5) below, be a defence for the person charged to prove that he took all reasonable precautions and exercised all due diligence to avoid the commission of the offence by himself or by a person under his control.

(2) Without prejudice to the generality of subsection (1) above, a person charged with an offence under section 8, 14 or 15 above who neither –

(a) prepared the food in respect of which the offence is alleged to have been committed; nor

(b) imported it into Great Britain,

shall be taken to have established the defence provided by that subsection if he satisfies the requirements of subsection (3) or (4) below.

(3) A person satisfies the requirements of this subsection if he proves –

(a) that the commission of the offence was due to an act or default of another person who was not under his control, or to reliance on information supplied by such a person;

(b) that he carried out all such checks of the food in question as were reasonable in all the circumstances, or that it was reasonable in all the circumstances for him to rely on checks carried out by the person who supplied the food to him; and

(c) that he did not know and had no reason to suspect at the time of the commission of the alleged offence that his act or omission would amount to an offence under the relevant provision.

(4) A person satisfies the requirements of this subsection if he proves –

(a) that the commission of the offence was due to an act or default of another person who was not under his control, or to reliance on information supplied by such a person;

(b) that the sale or intended sale of which the alleged offence consisted was not a sale or intended sale under his name or mark; and

(c) that he did not know, and could not reasonably have been expected to know, at the time of the commission of the alleged offence that his act or omission would amount to an offence under the relevant provision.

(5) If in any case the defence provided by subsection (1) above involves the allegation that the commission of the offence was due to an act or default of another person, or to reliance on information supplied by another person, the person charged shall not, without leave of the court, be entitled to rely on that defence unless –

(a) at least seven clear days before the hearing; and

(b) where he has previously appeared before a court in connection with the alleged offence, within one month of his first such appearance,

he has served on the prosecutor a notice in writing giving such information identifying or assisting in the identification of that other person as was then in his possession.

(6) In subsection (5) above any reference to appearing before a court shall be construed as including a reference to being brought before a court.

22. In proceedings for an offence under any of the preceding provisions of this Part consisting of the advertisement for sale of any food, it shall be a defence for the person charged to prove –

(a) that he is a person whose business it is to publish or arrange for the publication of advertisements; and

(b) that he received the advertisement in the ordinary course of business and did not know and had no reason to suspect that its publication would amount to an offence under that provision.

Miscellaneous and supplemental

23. – (1) A food authority may provide, whether within or outside their area, training courses in food hygiene for persons who are or intend to become involved in food businesses, whether as proprietors or employees or otherwise.

(2) A food authority may contribute towards the expenses incurred under this section by any other such authority, or towards expenses incurred by any other person in providing, such courses as are mentioned in subsection (1) above.

24. – (1) A food authority may provide, whether within or outside their area, tanks or other apparatus for cleansing shellfish.

(2) A food authority may contribute towards the expenses incurred under this section by any other such authority, or towards expenses incurred by any other person in providing, and making available to the public tanks or other apparatus for cleansing shellfish.

(3) Nothing in this section authorises the establishment of any tank or other apparatus, or the execution of any other work, on, over or under tidal lands below high-water mark of ordinary spring tides, except in accordance with such plans and sections, and subject to such restrictions and conditions as may before the work is commenced be approved by the Secretary of State.

(4) In this section "cleansing", in relation to shellfish, includes subjecting them to any germicidal treatment.

25. – (1) For the purpose of facilitating the exercise of their functions under this Part, the Ministers may by order require every person who at the date of the order, or at any subsequent time, carries on a business of a specified class or description (in this section referred to as a "relevant business") –

    (a)   to afford to persons specified in the order such facilities for the taking of samples of any food, substance or contact material to which subsection (2) below applies; or

    (b)   to furnish to persons so specified such information concerning any such food, substance or contact material,

as (in each case) is specified in the order and is reasonably required by such persons.

(2) This subsection applies to –

    (a)   any food of a class specified in the order which is sold or intended to be sold in the course of a relevant business for human consumption;

    (b)   any substance of a class so specified which is sold in the course of such a business for use in the preparation of food for human consumption, or is used for that purpose in the course of such a business; and

    (c)   any contact material of a class so specified which is sold in the course of such a business and is intended to come into contact with food intended for human consumption.

(3) No information relating to any individual business which is obtained by means of an order under subsection (1) above shall, without the previous consent in writing of the person carrying on the business, be disclosed except –

    (a)   in accordance with directions of the Minister, so far as may be necessary for the purposes of this Act or of any corresponding enactment in force in Northern Ireland, or for the purpose of complying with any Community obligation; or

Appendix

    (b)   for the purposes of any proceedings for an offence against the order or any report of those proceedings;

and any person who discloses any such information in contravention of this subsection shall be guilty of an offence.

(4) In subsection (3) above the reference to a disclosure being necessary for the purposes of this Act includes a reference to it being necessary –

    (a)   for the purpose of securing that food complies with food safety requirements or in the interests of the public health; or

    (b)   for the purpose of protecting or promoting the interests of consumers;

and the reference to a disclosure being necessary for the purposes of any corresponding enactment in force in Northern Ireland shall be construed accordingly.

26. – (1) Regulations under this Part may –

    (a)   make provision for prohibiting or regulating the carrying out of commercial operations with respect to any food, food source or contact material –

        (i)   which fails to comply with the regulations; or

        (ii) in relation to which an offence against the regulations has been committed, or would have been committed if any relevant act or omission had taken place in Great Britain; and

    (b)   without prejudice to the generality of section 9 above, provide that any food which, in accordance with the regulations, is certified as being such food as is mentioned in paragraph (a) above may be treated for the purposes of that section as failing to comply with food safety requirements.

(2) Regulations under this Part may also –

    (a)   require persons carrying on any activity to which the regulations apply to keep and produce records and provide returns;

    (b)   prescribe the particulars to be entered on any register required to be kept in accordance with the regulations;

    (c)   require any such register to be open to inspection by the public at all reasonable times and, subject to that, authorise it to be kept by means of a computer;

    (d)   prescribe the periods for which and the conditions subject to which licences may be issued, and provide for the subsequent alteration of conditions and for the cancellation, suspension or revocation of licences;

    (e)   provide for an appeal to a magistrates' court or, in Scotland, to the sheriff, or to a tribunal constituted in accordance with the regulations, against any decision of an enforcement authority, or of an authorised officer of such an authority; and

    (f)   provide, as respects any appeal to such a tribunal, for the procedure on the appeal (including costs) and for any appeal against the tribunal's decision.

(3) Regulations under this Part or an order under section 25 above may –

    (a)   provide that an offence under the regulations or order shall be triable in such way as may be there specified; and

    (b)   include provisions under which a person guilty of such an offence shall be liable to such penalties (not exceeding those which may be imposed in respect of offences under this Act) as may be specified in the regulations or order.

PART III
Administration and Enforcement

Administration

27. – (1) Every authority to whom this section applies, that is to say, every food authority in England and Wales and every regional or islands council in Scotland, shall appoint in accordance with this section one or more persons (in this Act referred to as "public analysts") to act as analysts for the purpose of this Act within the authority's area.

(2) No person shall be appointed as a public analyst unless he possesses –

(a) such qualifications as may be prescribed by regulations made by the Ministers; or

(b) such other qualifications as the Ministers may approve,

and no person shall act as a public analyst for any area who is engaged directly or indirectly in any food business which is carried on in that area.

(3) An authority to whom this section applies shall pay to a public analyst such remuneration as may be agreed, which may be expressed to be payable either –

(a) in addition to any fees received by him under this Part; or

(b) on condition that any fees so received by him are paid over by him to the authority.

(4) An authority to whom this section applies who appoint only one public analyst may appoint also a deputy to act during any vacancy in the office of public analyst, or during the absence or incapacity of the holder of the office, and –

(a) the provisions of this section with respect to the qualifications, appointment, removal and remuneration of a public analyst shall apply also in relation to a deputy public analyst; and

(b) any reference in the following provisions of this Act to a public analyst shall be construed as including a reference to a deputy public analyst appointed under this subsection.

(5) In subsection (1) above "food authority" does not include the council of a non-metropolitan district, the Sub-Treasurer of the Inner Temple or the Under Treasurer of the Middle Temple; and in subsection (2) above the reference to being engaged directly or indirectly in a food business includes a reference to having made such arrangements with a food business as may be prescribed by regulations made by the Ministers.

28. – (1) A food authority, or a regional council in Scotland, may provide facilities for examinations for the purposes of this Act.

(2) In this Act "examination" means a microbiological examination and "examine" shall be construed accordingly.

Sampling and analysis etc

29. – An authorised officer of an enforcement authority may –

(a) purchase a sample of any food, or any substance capable of being used in the preparation of food;

(b) take a sample of any food, or any such substance, which –

    (i) appears to him to be intended for sale, or to have been sold, for human consumption; or

    (ii) is found by him on or in any premises which he is authorised to enter by or under section 32 below;

(c) take a sample from any food source, or a sample of any contact material, which is found by him on or in any such premises;

(d) take a sample of any article or substance which is found by him on or in any such premises and which he has reason to believe may be required as evidence in proceedings under any of the provisions of this Act or of regulations or orders made under it.

30. – (1) An authorised officer of an enforcement authority who has procured a sample under section 29 above shall –

(a) if he considers that the sample should be analysed, submit it to be analysed either –

    (i) by the public analyst for the area in which the sample was procured; or

    (ii) by the public analyst for the area which consists of or includes the area of the authority;

(b) if he considers that the sample should be examined, submit it to be examined by a food examiner.

(2) A person, other than such an officer, who has purchased any food, or any substance capable of being used in the preparation of food, may submit a sample of it –

(a) to be analysed by the public analyst for the area in which the purchase was made; or

(b) to be examined by a food examiner.

(3) If, in any case where a sample is proposed to be submitted for analysis under this section, the office of public analyst for the area in question is vacant, the sample shall be submitted to the public analyst for some other area.

(4) If, in any case where a sample is proposed to be or is submitted for analysis or examination under this section, the food analyst or examiner determines that he is for any reason unable to perform the analysis or examination, the sample shall be submitted or, as the case may be, sent by him to such other food analyst or examiner as he may determine.

(5) A food analyst or examiner shall analyse or examine as soon as practicable any sample submitted or sent to him under this section, but may, except where –

(a) he is the public analyst for the area in question; and

(b) the sample is submitted to him for analysis by an authorised officer of an enforcement authority,

demand in advance the payment of such reasonable fee as he may require.

(6) A food analyst or examiner who has analysed or examined a sample shall give to the person by whom it was submitted a certificate specifying the result of the analysis or examination.

(7) Any certificate given by a food analyst or examiner under subsection (6) above shall be signed by him, but the analysis or examination may be made by any person acting under his direction.

(8) In any proceedings under this Act, the production by one of the parties –

    (a)   of a document purporting to be a certificate given by a food analyst or examiner under subsection (6) above; or

    (b)   of a document supplied to him by the other party as being a copy of such a certificate,

shall be sufficient evidence of the facts stated in it unless, in a case falling within paragraph (a) above, the other party requires that the food analyst or examiner shall be called as a witness.

(9) In this section –

"food analyst" means a public analyst or any other person who possesses the requisite qualifications to carry out analyses for the purposes of this Act;

"food examiner" means any person who possesses the requisite qualifications to carry out examinations for the purposes of this Act;

"the requisite qualifications" means such qualifications as may be prescribed by regulations made by the Ministers, or such other qualifications as the Ministers may approve;

"sample", in relation to an authorised officer of an enforcement authority, includes any part of a sample retained by him in pursuance of regulations under section 31 below;

and where two or more public analysts are appointed for any area, any reference in this section to the public analyst for that area shall be construed as a reference to either or any of them.

31. – (1) The Ministers may by regulations make provision for supplementing or modifying the provisions of sections 29 and 30 above.

(2) Without prejudice to the generality of subsection (1) above, regulations under that subsection may make provision with respect to –

    (a)   the matters to be taken into account in determining whether, and at what times, samples should be procured;

    (b)   the manner of procuring samples, including the steps to be taken in order to ensure that any samples procured are fair samples;

    (c)   the method of dealing with samples, including (where appropriate) their division into parts;

    (d)   the persons to whom parts of samples are to be given and the persons by whom such parts are to be retained;

    (e)   the notices which are to be given to, and the information which is to be furnished by, the persons in charge of any food, substance, contact material or food source of or from which samples are procured;

    (f)   the methods which are to be used in analysing or examining samples, or parts of samples, or in classifying the results of analyses or examinations;

    (g)   the circumstances in which a food analyst or examiner is to be precluded, by reason of a conflict of interest, from analysing or examining a particular sample or part of a sample; and

    (h)   the circumstances in which samples, or parts of samples, are to be or may be submitted for analysis or examination –

(i) to the Government Chemist, or to such other food analyst or examiner as he may direct; or

(ii) to a person determined by or under the regulations.

(3) In this section "food analyst" and "food examiner" have the same meanings as in section 30 above.

Powers of entry and obstruction etc

32. – (1) An authorised officer of an enforcement authority shall, on producing, if so required, some duly authenticated document showing his authority, have a right at all reasonable hours –

(a) to enter any premises within the authority's area for the purpose of ascertaining whether there is or has been on the premises any contravention of the provisions of this Act, or of regulations or orders made under it; and

(b) to enter any business premises, whether within or outside the authority's area, for the purpose of ascertaining whether there is on the premises any evidence of any contravention within that area of any of such provisions; and

(c) in the case of an authorised officer of a food authority, to enter any premises for the purpose of the performance by the authority of their functions under this Act;

but admission to any premises used only as a private dwelling-house shall not be demanded as of right unless 24 hours' notice of the intended entry has been given to the occupier.

(2) If a justice of the peace, on sworn information in writing, is satisfied that there is reasonable ground for entry into any premises for any such purpose as is mentioned in subsection (1) above and either –

(a) that admission to the premises has been refused, or a refusal is apprehended, and that notice of the intention to apply for a warrant has been given to the occupier; or

(b) that an application for admission, or the giving of such a notice, would defeat the object of the entry, or that the case is one of urgency, or that the premises are unoccupied or the occupier temporarily absent,

the justice may by warrant signed by him authorise the authorised officer to enter the premises, if need be by reasonable force.

(3) Every warrant granted under this section shall continue in force for a period of one month.

(4) An authorised officer entering any premises by virtue of this section, or of a warrant issued under it, may take with him such other persons as he considers necessary, and on leaving any unoccupied premises which he has entered by virtue of such a warrant shall leave them as effectively secured against unauthorised entry as he found them.

(5) An authorised officer entering premises by virtue of this section, or of a warrant issued under it, may inspect any records (in whatever form they are held) relating to a food business and, where any such records are kept by means of a computer –

(a) may have access to, and inspect and check the operation of, any computer and any associated apparatus or material which is or has been in use in connection with the records; and

    (b)   may require any person having charge of, or otherwise concerned with the operation of, the computer, apparatus or material to afford him such assistance as he may reasonably require.

(6) Any officer exercising any power conferred by subsection (5) above may –

    (a)   seize and detain any records which he has reason to believe may be required as evidence in proceedings under any of the provisions of this Act or of regulations or orders made under it; and

    (b)   where the records are kept by means of a computer, may require the records to be produced in a form in which they may be taken away.

(7) If any person who enters any premises by virtue of this section, or of a warrant issued under it, discloses to any person any information obtained by him in the premises with regard to any trade secret, he shall, unless the disclosure was made in the performance of his duty, be guilty of an offence.

(8) Nothing in this section authorises any person, except with the permission of the local authority under the Animal Health Act 1981, to enter any premises –

    (a)   in which an animal or bird affected with any disease to which that Act applies is kept; and

    (b)   which is situated in a place declared under that Act to be infected with such a disease.

(9) In the application of this section to Scotland, any reference to a justice of the peace includes a reference to the sheriff and to a magistrate.

33. – (1) Any person who –

    (a)   intentionally obstructs any person acting in the execution of this Act; or

    (b)   without reasonable cause, fails to give to any person acting in the execution of this Act any assistance or information which that person may reasonably require of him for the performance of his functions under this Act,

shall be guilty of an offence.

(2) Any person who, in purported compliance with any such requirement as is mentioned in subsection (1)(b) above –

    (a)   furnishes information which he knows to be false or misleading in a material particular; or

    (b)   recklessly furnishes information which is false or misleading in a material particular,

shall be guilty of an offence.

(3) Nothing in subsection (1)(b) above shall be construed as requiring any person to answer any question or give any information if to do so might incriminate him.

Offences

34. No prosecution for an offence under this Act which is punishable under section 35(2) below shall be begun after the expiry of –

    (a)   three years from the commission of the offence; or

    (b)   one year from its discovery by the prosecutor,

whichever is the earlier.

35. – (1) A person guilty of an offence under section 33(1) above shall be liable on summary conviction to a fine not exceeding level 5 on the standard scale or to imprisonment for a term not exceeding three months or to both.

(2) A person guilty of any other offence under this Act shall be liable –

(a) on conviction on indictment, to a fine or to imprisonment for a term not exceeding two years or to both;

(b) on summary conviction, to a fine not exceeding the relevant amount or to imprisonment for a term not exceeding six months or to both.

(3) In subsection (2) above "the relevant amount" means –

(a) in the case of an offence under section 7, 8 or 14 above, £20,000;

(b) in any other case, the statutory maximum.

(4) If a person who is –

(a) licensed under section 1 of the Slaughterhouses Act 1974 to keep a slaughterhouse or knacker's yard;

(b) registered under section 4 of the Slaughter of Animals (Scotland) Act 1980 in respect of any premises for use as a slaughterhouse; or

(c) licensed under section 6 of that Act to use any premises as a knacker's yard,

is convicted of an offence under Part II of this Act, the court may, in addition to any other punishment, cancel his licence or registration.

36. – (1) Where an offence under this Act which has been committed by a body corporate is proved to have been committed with the consent or connivance of, or to be attributable to any neglect on the part of –

(a) any director, manager, secretary or other similar officer of the body corporate; or

(b) any person who was purporting to act in any such capacity,

he as well as the body corporate shall be deemed to be guilty of that offence and shall be liable to be proceeded against and punished accordingly.

(2) In subsection (1) above "director", in relation to any body corporate established by or under any enactment for the purpose of carrying on under national ownership any industry or part of an industry or undertaking, being a body corporate whose affairs are managed by its members, means a member of that body corporate.

Appeals

37. – (1) Any person who is aggrieved by –

(a) a decision of an authorised officer of an enforcement authority to serve an improvement notice;

(b) a decision of an enforcement authority to refuse to issue such a certificate as is mentioned in section 11(6) or 12(8) above; or

(c) subject to subsection (2) below, a decision of such an authority to refuse, cancel, suspend or revoke a licence required by regulations under Part II of this Act,

may appeal to a magistrates' court or, in Scotland, to the sheriff.

(2) Subsection (1)(c) above shall not apply in relation to any decision as respects which regulations under Part II of this Act provide for an appeal to a tribunal constituted in accordance with the regulations.

(3) The procedure on an appeal to a magistrates' court under subsection (1) above, or an appeal to such a court for which provision is made by regulations under Part II of this Act, shall be by way of complaint for an order, and the Magistrates' Courts Act 1980 shall apply to the proceedings.

(4) An appeal to the sheriff under subsection (1) above, or an appeal to the sheriff for which provision is made by regulations under Part II of this Act, shall be by summary application.

(5) The period within which such an appeal as is mentioned in subsection (3) or (4) above may be brought shall be –

    (a)   one month from the date on which notice of the decision was served on the person desiring to appeal; or

    (b)   in the case of an appeal under subsection (1)(a) above, that period or the period specified in the improvement notice, whatever ends the earlier;

and, in the case of such an appeal as is mentioned in subsection (3) above, the making of the complaint shall be deemed for the purposes of this subsection to be the bringing of the appeal.

(6) In any case where such an appeal as is mentioned in subsection (3) or (4) above lies, the document notifying the decision to the person concerned shall state –

    (a)   the right of appeal to a magistrates' court or to the sheriff; and

    (b)   the period within which such an appeal may be brought.

38. – A person who is aggrieved by –

    (a)   any dismissal by a magistrates' court of such an appeal as is mentioned in section 37(3) above; or

    (b)   any decision of such a court to make a prohibition order or an emergency prohibition order, or to exercise the power conferred by section 35(4) above,

may appeal to the Crown Court.

39. – (1) On an appeal against an improvement notice, the court may either cancel or affirm the notice and, if it affirms it, may do so either in its original form or with such modifications as the court may in the circumstances think fit.

(2) Where, apart from this subsection, any period specified in an improvement notice would include any day on which an appeal against that notice is pending, that day shall be excluded from that period.

(3) An appeal shall be regarded as pending for the purposes of subsection (2) above until it is finally disposed of, is withdrawn or is struck out for want of prosecution.

PART IV
Miscellaneous and Supplemental

Powers of Ministers

40. – (1) For the guidance of food authorities, the Ministers or the Minister may issue codes of recommended practice as regards the execution and enforcement of this Act and of regulations and orders made under it; and any such code shall be laid before Parliament after being issued.

(2) In the exercise of the functions conferred on them by or under this Act, every food authority –

    (a)   shall have regard to any relevant provision of any such code; and

    (b)   shall comply with any direction which is given by the Ministers or the Minister and requires them to take any specified steps in order to comply with such a code.

(3) Any direction under subsection (2)(b) above shall, on the application of the Ministers or the Minister, be enforceable by mandamus or, in Scotland, by an order of the Court of Session under section 45 of the Court of Session Act 1988.

(4) Before issuing any code under this section, the Ministers or the Minister shall consult with such organisations as appear to them or him to be representative of interests likely to be substantially affected by the code.

(5) Any consultation undertaken before the commencement of subsection (4) above shall be as effective, for the purposes of that subsection, as if undertaken after that commencement.

41. Every food authority shall send to the Minister such reports and returns, and give him such information, with respect to the exercise of the functions conferred on them by or under this Act as he may require.

42. – (1) Where the Minister is satisfied that –

    (a)   a food authority (in this section referred to as "the authority in default") have failed to discharge any duty imposed by or under this Act; and

    (b)   the authority's failure affects the general interests of consumers of food,

he may by order empower another food authority (in this section referred to as "the substitute authority"), or one of his officers, to discharge that duty in place of the authority in default.

(2) For the purpose of determining whether the power conferred by subsection (1) above is exercisable, the Minister may cause a local inquiry to be held; and where he does so, the relevant provisions of the Local Government Act shall apply as if the inquiry were a local inquiry held under that Act.

(3) Nothing in subsection (1) above affects any other power exercisable by the Minister with respect to defaults of local authorities.

(4) The substitute authority or the Minister may recover from the authority in default any expenses reasonably incurred by them or him under subsection (1) above; and for the purpose of paying any such amount the authority in default may –

(a)   raise money as if the expenses had been incurred directly by them as a local authority; and

(b)   if and to the extent that they are authorised to do so by the Minister, borrow money in accordance with the statutory provisions relating to borrowing by a local authority.

(5) In this section "the relevant provisions of the Local Government Act" means subsections (2) to (5) of section 250 of the Local Government Act 1972 in relation to England and Wales and subsections (3) to (8) of section 210 of the Local Government (Scotland) Act 1973 in relation to Scotland.

Protective provisions

43. – (1) This section shall have effect on the death of any person who –

(a)   is registered in respect of any premises in accordance with regulations made under Part II of this Act; or

(b)   holds a licence issued in accordance with regulations so made.

(2) The registration or licence shall subsist for the benefit of the deceased's personal representative, or his widow or any other member of his family, until the end of –

(a)   the period of three months beginning with his death; or

(b)   such longer period as the enforcement authority may allow.

44. – (1) An officer of a food authority is not personally liable in respect of any act done by him –

(a)   in the execution or purported execution of this Act; and

(b)   within the scope of his employment,

if he did that act in the honest belief that his duty under this Act required or entitled him to do it.

(2) Nothing in subsection (1) above shall be construed as relieving any food authority from any liability in respect of the acts of their officers.

(3) Where an action has been brought against an officer of a food authority in respect of an act done by him –

(a)   in the execution or purported execution of this Act; but

(b)   outside the scope of his employment,

the authority may indemnify him against the whole or a part of any damages which he has been ordered to pay or any costs which he may have incurred if they are satisfied that he honestly believed that the act complained of was within the scope of his employment.

(4) A public analyst appointed by a food authority shall be treated for the purposes of this section as being an officer of the authority, whether or not his appointment is a whole-time appointment.

Financial provisions

45. – (1) The Ministers may make regulations requiring or authorising charges to be imposed by enforcement authorities in respect of things done by them which they are required or authorised to do by or under this Act.

(2) Regulations under this section may include such provision as the Ministers see fit as regards charges for which the regulations provide and the recovery of such charges; and nothing in the following provisions shall prejudice this.

(3) Regulations under this section may provide that the amount of a charge (if imposed) is to be at the enforcement authority's discretion or to be at its discretion subject to a maximum or a minimum.

(4) Regulations under this section providing that a charge may not exceed a maximum amount, or be less than a minimum amount, may –

    (a) provide for one amount, or a scale of amounts to cover different prescribed cases; and

    (b) prescribe, as regards any amount, a sum or a method of calculating the amount.

46. – (1) Any expenses which are incurred under this Act by an authorised officer of a food authority in procuring samples, and causing samples to be analysed or examined, shall be defrayed by that authority.

(2) Any expenses incurred by a county council in the enforcement and execution of any provision of this Act, or of any regulations or orders made under it, shall, if the Secretary of State so directs, be defrayed as expenses for special county purposes charged on such part of the county as may be specified in the direction.

47. There shall be paid out of money provided by Parliament to the chairman of any tribunal constituted in accordance with regulations under this Act such remuneration (by way of salary or fees) and such allowances as the Ministers may with the approval of the Treasury determine.

Instruments and documents

48. – (1) Any power of the Ministers or the Minister to make regulations or an order under this Act includes power –

    (a) to apply, with modifications and adaptations, any other enactment (including one contained in this Act) which deals with matters similar to those being dealt with by the regulations or order;

    (b) to make different provision in relation to different cases or classes of case (including different provision for different areas or different classes of business); and

    (c) to provide for such exceptions, limitations and conditions, and to make such supplementary, incidental, consequential or transitional provisions, as the Ministers or the Minister considers necessary or expedient.

(2) Any powers of the Ministers or the Minister to make regulations or orders under this Act shall be exercisable by statutory instrument.

(3) Any statutory instrument containing –

    (a) regulations under this Act; or

    (b) an order under this Act other than an order under section 60(3) below,

shall be subject to annulment in pursuance of a resolution of either House of Parliament.

(4) Before making –

(a) any regulations under this Act, other than regulations under section 17(2) or 18(1)(c) above; or

(b) any order under Part I of this Act,

the Ministers shall consult with such organisations as appear to them to be representative of interests likely to be substantially affected by the regulations or order.

(5) Any consultation undertaken before the commencement of subsection (4) above shall be as effective, for the purposes of that subsection, as if undertaken after that commencement.

49. – (1) The following shall be in writing, namely –

(a) all documents authorised or required by or under this Act to be given, made or issued by a food authority; and

(b) all notices and applications authorised or required by or under this Act to be given or made to, or to any officer of, such an authority.

(2) The Ministers may by regulations prescribe the form of any document to be used for any of the purposes of this Act and, if forms are so prescribed, those forms or forms to the like effect may be used in all cases to which those forms are applicable.

(3) Any document which a food authority are authorised or required by or under this Act to give, make or issue may be signed on behalf of the authority –

(a) by the proper officer of the authority as respects documents relating to matters within his province; or

(b) by any officer of the authority authorised by them in writing to sign documents of the particular kind or, as the case may be, the particular document.

(4) Any document purporting to bear the signature of an officer who is expressed –

(a) to hold an office by virtue of which he is under this section empowered to sign such a document; or

(b) to be duly authorised by the food authority to sign such a document or the particular document,

shall for the purposes of this Act, and of any regulations and orders made under it, be deemed, until the contrary is proved, to have been duly given, made or issued by authority of the food authority.

(5) In this section –

"proper officer", in relation to any purpose and to any food authority or any area, means the officer appointed for that purpose by that authority or, as the case may be, for that area;

"signature" includes a facsimile of a signature by whatever process reproduced.

50. – (1) Any document which is required or authorised by or under this Act to be given to or served on any person may, in any case for which no other provision is made by this Act, be given or served either –

(a) by delivering it to that person;

(b) in the case of any officer of an enforcement authority, by leaving it, or sending it in a prepaid letter addressed to him, at his office;

(c) in the case of an incorporated company or body, by delivering it to their secretary or clerk at their registered or principal office, or by sending it in a prepaid letter addressed to him at that office; or

(d) in the case of any other person, by leaving it, or sending it in a prepaid letter addressed to him, at his usual or last known residence.

(2) Where a document is to be given to or served on the owner or the occupier of any premises and it is not practicable after reasonable inquiry to ascertain the name and address of the person to or on whom it should be given or served, or the premises are unoccupied, the document may be given or served by addressing it to the person concerned by the description of "owner" or "occupier" of the premises (naming them) and –

(a) by delivering it to some person on the premises; or

(b) if there is no person on the premises to whom it can be delivered, by affixing it, or a copy of it, to some conspicuous part of the premises.

Amendments of other Acts

51. – (1) Part I of the Food and Environment Protection Act 1985 (contamination of food) shall have effect, and shall be deemed always to have had effect, subject to the amendments specified in subsection (2) below.

(2) The amendments referred to in subsection (1) above are –

(a) in subsection (1) of section 1 (power to make emergency orders), the substitution for paragraph (a) of the following paragraph –

"(a) there exist or may exist circumstances which are likely to create a hazard to human health through human consumption of food";

(b) in subsection (2) of that section, the omission of the definition of "escape";

(c) the substitution for subsection (5) of that section of the following subsection –

"(5) An emergency order shall refer to the circumstances or suspected circumstances in consequence of which in the opinion of the designating authority making it food such as is mentioned in subsection (1)(b) above is, or may be, or may become, unsuitable for human consumption; and in this Act 'designated circumstances' means the circumstances or suspected circumstances to which an emergency order refers in pursuance of this subsection.";

(d) in section 2(3) (powers when emergency order has been made), the substitution for the words "a designated incident" of the words "designated circumstances";

(e) in paragraph (a) of subsection (1) of section 4 (powers of officers), the substitution for the words "an escape of substances" of the words "such circumstances as are mentioned in section 1(1) above"; and

(f) in paragraphs (b) and (c) of that subsection, the substitution for the words "the designated incident" of the words "the designated circumstances".

52. – In the Food Act 1984 (in this Act referred to as "the 1984 Act") –

(a) Part III (markets); and

(b)   Part V (sugar beet and cold storage),

shall have effect subject to the amendments specified in Schedule 2 to this Act.

Supplemental

53. – (1) In this Act, unless the context otherwise requires –

"the 1984 Act" means the Food Act 1984;

"the 1956 Act" means the Food and Drugs (Scotland) Act 1956;

"advertisement" includes any notice, circular, label, wrapper, invoice or other document, and any public announcement made orally or by any means of producing or transmitting light or sound, and "advertise" shall be construed accordingly;

"analysis" includes microbiological assay and any technique for establishing the composition of food, and "analyse" shall be construed accordingly;

"animal" means any creature other than a bird or fish;

"article" does not include a live animal or bird, or a live fish which is not used for human consumption while it is alive;

"container" includes any basket, pail, tray, package or receptacle of any kind, whether open or closed;

"contravention", in relation to any provision, includes any failure to comply with that provision;

"cream" means that part of milk rich in fat which has been separated by skimming or otherwise;

"equipment" includes any apparatus;

"exportation" and "importation" have the same meanings as they have for the purposes of the Customs and Excise Management Act 1979, and "export" and "import" shall be construed accordingly;

"fish" includes crustaceans and molluscs;

"functions" includes powers and duties;

"human consumption" includes use in the preparation of food for human consumption;

"knacker's yard" means any premises used in connection with the business of slaughtering, flaying or cutting up animals the flesh of which is not intended for human consumption;

"milk" includes cream and skimmed or separated milk;

"occupier", in relation to any ship or aircraft of a description specified in an order made under section 1(3) above or any vehicle, stall or place, means the master, commander or other person in charge of the ship, aircraft, vehicle, stall or place;

"officer" includes servant;

"preparation", in relation to food, includes manufacture and any form of processing or treatment, and "preparation for sale" includes packaging, and "prepare for sale" shall be construed accordingly;

"presentation", in relation to food, includes the shape, appearance and packaging of the food, the way in which the food is arranged when it is exposed for sale and the setting in which the food is displayed with a view to sale, but does not include any form of labelling or advertising, and "present" shall be construed accordingly;

"proprietor", in relation to a food business, means the person by whom that business is carried on;

Appendix

"ship" includes any vessel, boat or craft, and a hovercraft within the meaning of the Hovercraft Act 1968, and "master" shall be construed accordingly;

"slaughterhouse" means a place for slaughtering animals, the flesh of which is intended for sale for human consumption, and includes any place available in connection with such a place for the confinement of animals while awaiting slaughter there or for keeping, or subjecting to any treatment or process, products of the slaughtering of animals there;

"substance" includes any natural or artificial substance or other matter, whether it is in solid or liquid form or in the form of a gas or vapour;

"treatment", in relation to food, includes subjecting it to heat or cold.

(2) The following Table shows provisions defining or otherwise explaining expressions used in this Act (other than provisions defining or explaining an expression used only in the same section) –

authorised officer of a food authority	section 5(6)
business	section 1(3)
commercial operation	section 1(3) and (4)
contact material	section 1(3)
emergency control order	section 13(1)
emergency prohibition notice	section 12(1)
emergency prohibition order	section 12(2)
enforcement authority	section 6(1)
examination and examine	section 28(2)
food	section 1(1), (2) and (4)
food authority	section 5
food business	section 1(3)
food premises	section 1(3)
food safety requirements and related expressions	section 8(2)
food source	section 1(3)
improvement notice	section 10(1)
injury to health and injurious to health	section 7(3)
the Minister	section 4(1) and (2)
the Ministers	section 4(1)
premises	section 1(3)
prohibition order	section 11(5)
public analyst	section 27(1)
sale and related expressions	section 2
unfit for human consumption	section 8(4)

(3) Any reference in this Act to regulations or orders made under it shall be construed as a reference to regulations or orders made under this Act by the Ministers or the Minister.

(4) For the purposes of this Act, any class or description may be framed by reference to any matters or circumstances whatever, including in particular, in the case of a description of food, the brand name under which it is commonly sold.

137

(5) Where, apart from this subsection, any period of less than seven days which is specified in this Act would include any day which is –

    (a)   a Saturday, a Sunday, Christmas Day or Good Friday; or

    (b)   a day which is a bank holiday under the Banking and Financial Dealings Act 1971 in the part of Great Britain concerned,

that day shall be excluded from that period.

54. – (1) Subject to the provisions of this section, the provisions of this Act and of regulations and orders made under it shall bind the Crown.

(2) No contravention by the Crown of any provision of this Act or of any regulations or order made under it shall make the Crown criminally liable; but the High Court or, in Scotland, the Court of Session may, on the application of an enforcement authority, declare unlawful any act or omission of the Crown which constitutes such a contravention.

(3) Notwithstanding anything in subsection (2) above, the provisions of this Act and of regulations and orders made under it shall apply to persons in the public service of the Crown as they apply to other persons.

(4) If the Secretary of State certifies that it appears to him requisite or expedient in the interests of national security that the powers of entry conferred by section 32 above should not be exercisable in relation to any Crown premises specified in the certificate, those powers shall not be exercisable in relation to those premises; and in this subsection "Crown premises" means premises held or used by or on behalf of the Crown.

(5) Nothing in this section shall be taken as in any way affecting Her Majesty in her private capacity; and this subsection shall be construed as if section 38(3) of the Crown Proceedings Act 1947 (interpretation of references in that Act to Her Majesty in her private capacity) were contained in this Act.

55. – (1) Nothing in Part II of this Act or any regulations or order made under that Part shall apply in relation to the supply of water to any premises, whether by a water undertaker or by means of a private supply (within the meaning of Chapter II of Part II of the Water Act 1989).

(2) In the following provisions of that Act, namely –

section 52 (duties of water undertakers with respect to water quality);

section 53 (regulations for preserving water quality); and

section 64 (additional powers of entry for the purposes of Chapter II),

for the words "domestic purposes", wherever they occur, there shall be substituted the words "domestic or food production purposes".

(3) In subsection (2) of section 56 of that Act (general functions of local authorities in relation to water quality), for the words "domestic purposes" there shall be substituted the words "domestic or food production purposes" and for the words "those purposes" there shall be substituted the words "domestic purposes".

(4) In subsection (1) of section 57 of that Act (remedial powers of local authorities in relation to private supplies), for the words "domestic purposes", in the first place where they occur, there shall be substituted the words "domestic or food production purposes".

(5) In subsection (1) of section 66 of that Act (interpretation etc. of Chapter II), after the definition of "consumer" there shall be inserted the following definition –

    " 'food production purposes' shall be construed in accordance with subsection (1A) below;".

(6) After that subsection there shall be inserted the following subsection –

"(1A) In this Chapter references to food production purposes are references to the manufacturing, processing, preserving or marketing purposes with respect to food or drink for which water supplied to food production premises may be used; and in this subsection 'food production premises' means premises used for the purposes of a business of preparing food or drink for consumption otherwise than on the premises."

56. – (1) Nothing in Part II of this Act or any regulations or order made under that Part shall apply in relation to the supply of water to any premises, whether by a water authority (within the meaning of section 3 of the Water (Scotland) Act 1980) or by means of a private supply (within the meaning of Part VIA of that Act).

(2) In the following provisions of that Act, namely –

section 76A (duties of water authorities with respect to water quality); and

section 76B (regulations for preserving water quality),

for the words "domestic purposes", where they occur, there shall be substituted the words "domestic or food production purposes".

(3) In subsection (2) of section 76F of that Act (general functions of local authorities in relation to water quality), for the words "domestic purposes" there shall be substituted the words "domestic or food production purposes" and for the words "those purposes" there shall be substituted the words "domestic purposes".

(4) In subsection (1) of section 76G of that Act (remedial powers of local authorities in relation to private supplies), for the words "domestic purposes", in the first place where they occur, there shall be substituted the words "domestic or food production purposes".

(5) In subsection (1) of section 76L of that Act (interpretation etc. of Part VIA), after the definition of "analyse" there shall be inserted the following definition –

" 'food production purposes' shall be construed in accordance with subsection (1A) below;".

(6) After that subsection there shall be inserted the following subsection –

"(1A) In this Part references to food production purposes are references to the manufacturing, processing, preserving or marketing purposes with respect to food or drink for which water supplied to food production premises may be used; and in this subsection 'food production premises' means premises used for the purposes of a business of preparing food or drink for consumption otherwise than on the premises."

57. – (1) This Act shall apply to the Isles of Scilly, subject to such exceptions and modifications as the Ministers may by order direct.

(2) Her Majesty may by Order in Council direct that any of the provisions of this Act shall extend to any of the Channel Islands with such exceptions and modifications (if any) as may be specified in the Order.

58. – (1) For the purposes of this Act the territorial waters of the United Kingdom adjacent to any part of Great Britain shall be treated as situated in that part.

(2) An Order in Council under section 23 of the Oil and Gas (Enterprise) Act 1982 (application of civil law) may make provision for treating for the purposes of food safety legislation –

(a)   any installation which is in waters to which that section applies; and

(b)   any safety zone around any such installation,

as if they were situated in a specified part of the United Kingdom and for modifying such legislation in its application to such installations and safety zones.

(3) Such an Order in Council may also confer on persons of a specified description the right to require, for the purpose of facilitating the exercise of specified powers under food safety legislation –

(a)   conveyance to and from any installation, including conveyance of any equipment required by them; and

(b)   the provision of reasonable accommodation and means of subsistence while they are on any installation.

(4) In this section –

"food safety legislation" means this Act and any regulations and orders made under it and any corresponding provisions in Northern Ireland;

"installation" means an installation to which subsection (3) of the said section 23 applies;

"safety zone" means an area which is a safety zone by virtue of Part III of the Petroleum Act 1987; and

"specified" means specified in the Order in Council.

59. – (1) The enactments mentioned in Schedule 3 to this Act shall have effect subject to the amendments there specified (being minor amendments and amendments consequential on the preceding provisions of this Act).

(2) The Ministers may by order make such modifications of local Acts, and of subordinate legislation (within the meaning of the Interpretation Act 1978), as appear to them to be necessary or expedient in consequence of the provisions of this Act.

(3) The transitional provisions and savings contained in Schedule 4 to this Act shall have effect; but nothing in this subsection shall be taken as prejudicing the operation of sections 16 and 17 of the said Act of 1978 (which relate to the effect of repeals).

(4) The enactments mentioned in Schedule 5 to this Act (which include some that are spent or no longer of practical utility) are hereby repealed to the extent specified in the third column of that Schedule.

60. – (1) This Act may be cited as the Food Safety Act 1990.

(2) The following provisions shall come into force on the day on which this Act is passed, namely –

section 13;

section 51; and

paragraphs 12 to 15 of Schedule 2 and, so far as relating to those paragraphs, section 52.

(3) Subject to subsection (2) above, this Act shall come into force on such day as the Ministers may by order appoint, and different days may be appointed for different provisions or for different purposes.

(4) An order under subsection (3) above may make such transitional adaptations of any of the following, namely –

(a)   the provisions of this Act then in force or brought into force by the order; and (b)　the provisions repealed by this Act whose repeal is not then in force or so brought into force,

as appear to the Ministers to be necessary or expedient in consequence of the partial operation of this Act.

(5) This Act, except –

this section;

section 51;

section 58(2) or (4); and

paragraphs 7, 29 and 30 of Schedule 3 and, so far as relating to those paragraphs, section 59(1),

does not extend to Northern Ireland.

Schedules

SCHEDULE 1
Provisions of Regulations under section 16(1)

Composition of food

1. Provision for prohibiting or regulating –

(a)　the sale, possession for sale, or offer, exposure or advertisement for sale, of any specified substance, or of any substance of any specified class, with a view to its use in the preparation of food; or

(b)　the possession of any such substance for use in the preparation of food.

Fitness etc of food

2. – (1) Provision for prohibiting –

(a)　the sale for human consumption; or

(b)　the use in the manufacture of products for sale for such consumption,

of food derived from a food source which is suffering or has suffered from, or which is liable to be suffering or to have suffered from, any disease specified in the regulations.

(2) Provision for prohibiting or regulating, or for enabling enforcement authorities to prohibit or regulate –

(a)　the sale for human consumption; or

(b)　the offer, exposure or distribution for sale for such consumption,

of shellfish taken from beds or other layings for the time being designated by or under the regulations.

3. – (1) Provision for regulating generally the treatment and disposal of any food –

    (a)   which is unfit for human consumption; or

    (b)   which, though not unfit for human consumption, is not intended for, or is prohibited from being sold for, such consumption.

(2) Provision for the following, namely –

    (a)   for the registration by enforcement authorities of premises used or proposed to be used for the purpose of sterilising meat to which sub-paragraph (1) above applies, and for prohibiting the use for that purpose of any premises which are not registered in accordance with the regulations; or

    (b)   for the issue by such authorities of licences in respect of the use of premises for the purpose of sterilising such meat, and for prohibiting the use for that purpose of any premises except in accordance with a licence issued under the regulations.

Processing and treatment of food

4. Provision for the following, namely –

    (a)   for the giving by persons possessing such qualifications as may be prescribed by the regulations of written opinions with respect to the use of any process or treatment in the preparation of food, and for prohibiting the use for any such purpose of any process or treatment except in accordance with an opinion given under the regulations; or

    (b)   for the issue by enforcement authorities of licences in respect of the use of any process or treatment in the preparation of food, and for prohibiting the use for any such purpose of any process or treatment except in accordance with a licence issued under the regulations.

Food hygiene

5. – (1) Provision for imposing requirements as to –

    (a)   the construction, maintenance, cleanliness and use of food premises, including any parts of such premises in which equipment and utensils are cleaned, or in which refuse is disposed of or stored;

    (b)   the provision, maintenance and cleanliness of sanitary and washing facilities in connection with such premises; and

    (c)   the disposal of refuse from such premises.

(2) Provision for imposing requirements as to –

    (a)   the maintenance and cleanliness of equipment or utensils used for the purposes of a food business; and

    (b)   the use, for the cleaning of equipment used for milking, of cleaning agents approved by or under the regulations.

(3) Provision for requiring persons who are or intend to become involved in food businesses, whether as proprietors or employees or otherwise, to undergo such food hygiene training as may be specified in the regulations.

6. – (1) Provision for imposing responsibility for compliance with any requirements imposed by virtue of paragraph 5(1) above in respect of any premises –

(a) on the occupier of the premises; and

(b) in the case of requirements of a structural character, on any owner of the premises who either –

(i) lets them for use for a purpose to which the regulations apply; or

(ii) permits them to be so used after notice from the authority charged with the enforcement of the regulations.

(2) Provision for conferring in relation to particular premises, subject to such limitations and safeguards as may be specified, exemptions from the operation of specified provisions which –

(a) are contained in the regulations; and

(b) are made by virtue of paragraph 5(1) above,

while there is in force a certificate of the enforcement authority to the effect that compliance with those provisions cannot reasonably be required with respect to the premises or any activities carried on in them.

Inspection etc of food sources

7. – (1) Provision for securing the inspection of food sources by authorised officers of enforcement authorities for the purpose of ascertaining whether they –

(a) fail to comply with the requirements of the regulations; or

(b) are such that any food derived from them is likely to fail to comply with those requirements.

(2) Provisions for enabling such an officer, if it appears to him on such an inspection that any food source falls within sub-paragraph (1)(a) or (b) above, to give notice to the person in charge of the food source that, until a time specified in the notice or until the notice is withdrawn –

(a) no commercial operations are to be carried out with respect to the food source; and

(b) the food source either is not to be removed or is not to be removed except to some place so specified.

(3) Provision for enabling such an officer, if on further investigation it appears to him, in the case of any such food source which is a live animal or bird, that there is present in the animal or bird any substance whose presence is prohibited by the regulations, to cause the animal or bird to be slaughtered.

SCHEDULE 2
Amendments of Parts III and V of 1984 Act

Amendments of Part III

1. Part III of the 1984 Act (markets) shall be amended in accordance with paragraphs 2 to 11 below.

2. – (1) In subsection (1) of section 50 (establishment or acquisition of markets), for the words "The council of a district" there shall be substituted the words "A local authority" and for the words "their district", in each place where they occur, there shall be substituted the words "their area".

(2) In subsection (2) of that section, for the words "the district" there shall be substituted the words "the authority's area".

(3) For subsection (3) of that section there shall be substituted the following subsection –

"(3) For the purposes of subsection (2), a local authority shall not be regarded as enjoying any rights, powers or privileges within another local authority's area by reason only of the fact that they maintain within their own area a market which has been established under paragraph (a) of subsection (1) or under the corresponding provision of any earlier enactment".

3. In section 51(2) (power to sell to local authority), the word "market" shall cease to have effect.

4. – (1) In subsection (1) of section 53 (charges by market authority), the words "and in respect of the weighing and measuring of articles and vehicles" shall cease to have effect.

(2) For subsection (2) of that section there shall be substituted the following subsection –

"(2) A market authority who provide –
    (a) a weighing machine for weighing cattle, sheep or swine; or
    (b) a cold store or refrigerator for the storage and preservation of meat and
        other articles of food,
may demand in respect of the weighing of such animals or, as the case may be, the use of the store or refrigerator such charges as they may from time to time determine."

(3) In subsection (3)(b) of that section, the words "in respect of the weighing of vehicles, or, as the case may be," shall cease to have effect.

5. For subsection (2) of section 54 (time for payment of charges) there shall be substituted the following subsection –

"(2) Charges payable in respect of the weighing of cattle, sheep or swine shall be paid in advance to an authorised market officer by the person bringing the animals to be weighed."

6. In section 56(1) (prohibited sales in market hours), for the word "district" there shall be substituted the word "area".

7. In section 57 (weighing machines and scales), subsection (1) shall cease to have effect.

8. After that section there shall be inserted the following section –

"57A. – (1) A market authority may provide a cold air store or refrigerator for the storage and preservation of meat and other articles of food.

(2) Any proposal by a market authority to provide under this section a cold air store or refrigerator within the area of another local authority requires the consent of that other authority, which shall not be unreasonably withheld.

(3) Any question whether or not such a consent is unreasonably withheld shall be referred to and determined by the Ministers.

(4) Subsections (1) to (5) of section 250 of the Local Government Act 1972 (which relate to local inquiries) shall apply for the purposes of this section as if any reference in those subsections to that Act included a reference to this section."

9. Section 58 (weighing of articles) shall cease to have effect.

10. In section 60 (market byelaws), after paragraph (c) there shall be inserted the following paragraph –

"(d) after consulting the fire authority for the area in which the market is situated, for preventing the spread of fires in the market."

11. In section 61 (interpretation of Part III), the words from "and this Part" to the end shall cease to have effect and for the definition of "market authority" there shall be substituted the following definitions –

" 'fire authority' means an authority exercising the functions of a fire authority under the Fire Services Act 1947;

'food' has the same meaning as in the Food Safety Act 1990;

'local authority' means a district council, a London borough council or a parish or community council;

'market authority' means a local authority who maintain a market which has been established or acquired under section 50(1) or under the corresponding provisions of any earlier enactment."

Amendments of Part V

12. Part V of the 1984 Act (sugar beet and cold storage) shall be amended in accordance with paragraphs 13 to 16 below.

13. – (1) In subsections (1) and (2) of section 68 (research and education), for the word "Company", wherever it occurs, there shall be substituted the words "processors of home-grown beet".

(2) After subsection (5) of that section there shall be inserted the following subsection –

"(5A) An order under this section shall be made by statutory instrument which shall be subject to annulment in pursuance of a resolution of either House of Parliament.".

(3) In subsection (6) of that section, for the definition of "the Company" and subsequent definitions there shall be substituted –

" 'year' means a period of 12 months beginning with 1st April;
and in this section and section 69 and 69A 'home-grown beet' means sugar beet grown in Great Britain".

14. In subsection (3) of section 69 (crop price), for the words "'home-grown beet' means sugar beet grown in Great Britain; and" there shall be substituted the words "and section 69A".

15. After that section there shall be inserted the following section –

"69A. – (1) For the purpose of facilitating –

(a) the making of a determination under section 69(1); or

(b) the preparation or conduct of discussions concerning Community arrangements for or relating to the regulation of the market for sugar,

the appropriate Minister may serve on any processor of home-grown beet a notice requiring him to furnish in writing, within such period as specified in the notice, such information as is so specified.

(2) Subject to subsection (3), information obtained under subsection (1) shall not be disclosed without the previous consent in writing of the person by whom the information was furnished; and a person who discloses any information so obtained in contravention of this subsection shall be liable –

(a) on conviction on indictment, to a fine or to imprisonment for a term not exceeding two years or to both;

(b) on summary conviction, to a fine not exceeding the statutory maximum or to imprisonment for a term not exceeding three months or to both.

(3) Nothing in subsection (2) shall restrict the disclosure of information to any of the Ministers or the disclosure –

(a) of information obtained under subsection (1)(a) –

    (i) to a person designated to make a determination under section 69(1); or

    (ii) to a body which substantially represents the growers of home-grown beet; or

(b) of information obtained under subsection (1)(b), to the Community institution concerned.

(4) In this section "the appropriate Minister" means –

(a) in relation to England, the Minister of Agriculture, Fisheries and Food; and

(b) in relation to Scotland or Wales, the Secretary of State."

16. Section 70 (provision of cold storage) shall cease to have effect.

SCHEDULE 3
Minor and Consequential Amendments

The Public Health Act 1936 (c 49)

1. An order made by the Secretary of State under section 6 of the Public Health Act 1936 may constitute a united district for the purposes of any functions under this Act which are functions of a food authority in England and Wales.

Appendix

The London Government Act 1963 (c 33)

2. Section 54(1) of the London Government Act 1963 (food, drugs, markets and animals) shall cease to have effect.

The Agriculture Act 1967 (c 22)

3. In section 7(3) of the Agriculture Act 1967 (labelling of meat in relation to systems of classifying meat),the words from "and, without prejudice" to the end shall cease to have effect.

4. – (1) In subsection (2) of section 25 of that Act (interpretation of Part I), for the definition of "slaughterhouse" there shall be substituted the following definition –

"'slaughterhouse' has, in England and Wales, the meaning given by section 34 of the Slaughterhouses Act 1974 and, in Scotland, the meaning given by section 22 of the Slaughter of Animals (Scotland) Act 1980;".

(2) In subsection (3) of that section, for the words from "Part II" to "1955" there shall be substituted the words "section 15 of the Slaughterhouses Act 1974 or section 1 of the Slaughter of Animals (Scotland) Act 1980".

The Farm and Garden Chemicals Act 1967 (c 50)

5. In section 4 of the Farm and Garden Chemicals Act 1967 (evidence of analysis of products)—

    (a) in subsection (3), for the words "section 76 of the Food Act 1984" there shall be substituted the words "section 27 of the Food Safety Act 1990"; and

    (b) in subsection (7)(c), the words from "for the reference" to "1956" shall cease to have effect.

The Trade Descriptions Act 1968 (c 29)

6. In section 2(5)(a) of the Trade Descriptions Act 1968 (certain descriptions to be deemed not to be trade descriptions), for the words "the Food Act 1984, the Food and Drugs (Scotland) Act 1956" there shall be substituted the words "the Food Safety Act 1990".

7. In section 22 of that Act (admissibility of evidence in proceedings for offences under Act), in subsection (2), the paragraph beginning with the words "In this subsection" shall cease to have effect, and after that subsection there shall be inserted the following subsection –

"(2A) In subsection (2) of this section –

'the food and drugs laws' means the Food Safety Act 1990, the Medicines Act 1968 and the Food (Northern Ireland) Order 1989 and any instrument made thereunder;

'the relevant provisions' means –

    (i) in relation to the said Act of 1990, section 31 and regulations made thereunder;

(ii) in relation to the said Act of 1968, so much of Schedule 3 to that Act as is applicable to the circumstances in which the sample was procured; and

(iii) in relation to the said Order, Articles 40 and 44,

or any provisions replacing any of those provisions by virtue of section 17 of the said Act of 1990, paragraph 27 of Schedule 3 to the said Act of 1968 or Article 72 or 73 of the said Order."

The Medicines Act 1968 (c 67)

8. In section 108 of the Medicines Act 1968 (enforcement in England and Wales) –

(a) for the words "food and drugs authority", in each place where they occur, there shall be substituted the words "drugs authority"; and

(b) after subsection (11) there shall be inserted the following subsection –

"(12) In this section 'drugs authority' means –

(a) as respects each London borough, metropolitan district or non-metropolitan county, the council of that borough, district or county; and

(b) as respects the City of London (including the Temples), the Common Council of that City."

9. In section 109 of that Act (enforcement in Scotland) –

(a) paragraph (c) of subsection (2) shall cease to have effect; and

(b) after that subsection there shall be inserted the following subsection –

"(2A) Subsection (12) of section 108 of this Act shall have effect in relation to Scotland as if for paragraphs (a) and (b) there were substituted the words "an islands or district council".

10. After Section 115 of that Act there shall be inserted the following section –

"115A. A drugs authority or the council of a non-metropolitan district may provide facilities for microbiological examination of drugs."

11. In section 132(1) of that Act (interpretation), the definition of "food and drugs authority" shall cease to have effect and after the definition of "doctor" there shall be inserted the following definition—

" 'drugs authority' has the meaning assigned to it by section 108(12) of this Act;".

12. In paragraph 1(2) of Schedule 3 to that Act (sampling) for the words from "in relation to England and Wales" to "Food and Drugs (Scotland) Act 1956" there shall be substituted the words "except in relation to Northern Ireland, has the meaning assigned to it by section 27 of the Food Safety Act 1990".

The Transport Act 1968 (c 73)

13. In Schedule 16 to the Transport Act 1968 (supplementary and consequential provisions), in paragraph 7(2), paragraphs (d) and (e) shall cease to have effect.

Appendix

The Tribunals and Inquiries Act 1971 (c 62)

14. – (1) In Schedule 1 to the Tribunals and Inquiries Act 1971 (tribunals under supervision of Council on Tribunals),paragraph 15 shall cease to have effect and after paragraph 6B there shall be inserted the following paragraph –

"Food	6C. Tribunals constituted in accordance with regulations under Part II of the Food Safety Act 1990."

(2) In that Schedule, paragraph 40 shall cease to have effect and after paragraph 36 there shall be inserted the following paragraph –

"Food	36A. Tribunals constituted in accordance with regulations under Part II of the Food Safety Act 1990 being tribunals appointed for Scotland."

The Agriculture (Miscellaneous Provisions) Act 1972 (c 62)

15. – (1) In subsection (1) of section 4 of the Agriculture (Miscellaneous Provisions) Act 1972 (furnishing by milk marketing boards of information derived from tests of milk) –

    (a)   for the words "appropriate authority" there shall be substituted the words "enforcement authority"; and

    (b)   for the words from "Milk and Dairies Regulations" to "1956" there shall be substituted the words "regulations relating to milk, dairies or dairy farms which were made under, or have effect as if made under, section 16 of the Food Safety Act 1990."

(2) In subsection (2) of that section, for the definition of "appropriate authority" there shall be substituted the following definition –

" 'enforcement authority' has the same meaning as in the Food Safety Act 1990;".

(3) Subsection (3) of that section shall cease to have effect.

The Poisons Act 1972 (c 66)

16. In section 8(4)(a) of the Poisons Act 1972 (evidence of analysis in proceedings under Act) for the words "section 76 of the Food Act 1984, or section 27 of the Food and Drugs (Scotland) Act 1956" there shall be substituted the words "section 27 of the Food Safety Act 1990".

The Local Government Act 1972 (c 70)

17. In section 259(3) of the Local Government Act 1972 (compensation for loss of office) –

(a) in paragraph (b), for the words "food and drugs authority, within the meaning of the Food Act 1984" there shall be substituted the words "food authority within the meaning of the Food Safety Act 1990";

(b) in paragraph (c), for sub-paragraphs (i) and (ii) there shall be substituted the words "which are incorporated or reproduced in the Slaughterhouses Act 1974 or the Food Safety Act 1990"; and

(c) the words "section 129(1) of the Food and Drugs Act 1955" shall cease to have effect.

The Slaughterhouses Act 1974 (c 3)

18. In the following provisions of the Slaughterhouses Act 1974, namely—

(a) section 2(2)(a) (requirements to be complied with in relation to slaughterhouse licences);

(b) section 4(2)(a) (requirements to be complied with in relation to knacker's yard licences);

(c) section 12(2) (regulations with respect to slaughterhouses and knacker's yards to prevail over byelaws); and

(d) section 16(3) (regulations with respect to public slaughterhouses to prevail over byelaws),

for the words "section 13 of the Food Act 1984" there shall be substituted the words "section 16 of the Food Safety Act 1990".

The Licensing (Scotland) Act 1976 (c 66)

19. In section 23(4) of the Licensing (Scotland) Act 1976 (application for new licence), for the words "section 13 of the Food and Drugs (Scotland) Act 1956" there shall be substituted "section 16 of the Food Safety Act 1990".

The Weights and Measures etc Act 1976 (c 77)

20. – (1) In subsection (1) of section 12 of the Weights and Measures etc Act 1976 (shortages of food and other goods), for paragraphs (a) and (b) there shall be substituted the following paragraph –

"(a) section 16 of the Food Safety Act 1990 ('the 1990 Act');".

(2) In subsection (9) of that section –

(a) for paragraph (a) there shall be substituted the following paragraph –

"(a) where it was imposed under the 1990 Act –

(i) the Minister of Agriculture, Fisheries and Food and the Secretary of State acting jointly in so far as it was imposed in relation to England and Wales; and

(ii) the Secretary of State in so far as it was imposed in relation to Scotland;"; and

150

(b)   in paragraph (c), the words "the 1956 Act or" shall cease to have effect.

21. In Schedule 6 to that Act (temporary requirements imposed by emergency orders), for paragraphs 2 and 3 there shall be substituted the following paragraph –

"Food Safety Act 1990 (c 16)

2. – (1) This paragraph applies where the relevant requirement took effect under or by virtue of the Food Safety Act 1990.

(2) The following provisions of that Act –

(a)   Part I (preliminary);

(b)   Part III (administration and enforcement); and

(c)   sections 40 to 50 (default powers and other supplemental provisions),

shall apply as if the substituted requirement were imposed by regulations under section 16 of that Act."

The Hydrocarbon Oil Duties Act 1979 (c 5)

22. In Schedule 5 to the Hydrocarbon Oil Duties Act 1979 (sampling) in paragraph 5(d) for the words "section 76 of the Food Act 1984, section 27 of the Food and Drugs (Scotland) Act 1956" there shall be substituted the words "section 27 of the Food Safety Act 1990".

The Slaughter of Animals (Scotland) Act 1980 (c 13)

23. In section 19(2) of the Slaughter of Animals (Scotland) Act 1980 (enforcement) for the words "section 13 of the Food and Drugs (Scotland) Act 1956" there shall be substituted the words "section 16 of the Food Safety Act 1990" and for the words "section 36 of the said Act of 1956" there shall be substituted the words "section 32 of the said Act of 1990".

24. In section 22 of that Act (interpretation) –

(a)   for the definition of "knacker's yard" there shall be substituted the following definition –

" 'knacker's yard' means any premises used in connection with the business of slaughtering, flaying or cutting up animals the flesh of which is not intended for human consumption; and 'knacker' means a person whose business it is to carry out such slaughtering, flaying or cutting up"; and

(b)   for the definition of "slaughterhouse" there shall be substituted the following definition –

" 'slaughterhouse' means a place for slaughtering animals, the flesh of which is intended for human consumption, and includes any place available in connection with such a place for the confinement of animals while awaiting slaughter there or keeping, or subjecting to any treatment or process, products of the slaughtering of animals there; and 'slaughterman' means a person whose business it is to carry out such slaughtering".

The Civic Government (Scotland) Act 1982 (c 45)

25. In section 39 of the Civic Government (Scotland) Act 1982 (street traders' licences) –

(a) in subsection (3)(b), for the words "section 7 of the Milk and Dairies (Scotland) Act 1914" there shall be substituted the words "regulations made under section 19 of the Food Safety Act 1990"; and

(b) in subsection (4) –

   (i) for the words "regulations made under sections 13 and 56 of the Food and Drugs (Scotland) Act 1956", there shall be substituted the words "section 1(3) of the Food Safety Act 1990";

   (ii) for the words "islands or district council" there shall be substituted the words "food authority (for the purposes of section 5 of the Food Safety Act 1990)"; and

   (iii) for the words "sections 13 and 56 of the Food and Drugs (Scotland) Act 1956", there shall be substituted the words "section 16 of the Food Safety Act 1990".

The Public Health (Control of Disease) Act 1984 (c 22)

26. In section 3(2) of the Public Health (Control of Disease) Act 1984 (jurisdiction and powers of port health authority), for paragraph (a) there shall be substituted the following paragraph –

"(a) of a food authority under the Food Safety Act 1990;".

27. In section 7(3) of that Act (London port health authority), for paragraph (d) there shall be substituted the following paragraph –

"(d) of a food authority under any provision of the Food Safety Act 1990."

28. – (1) In subsection (1) of section 20 of that Act (stopping of work to prevent spread of disease), in paragraph (b) for the words "subsection (1) of section 28 of the Food Act 1984" there shall be substituted "subsection (1A) below".

(2) After that subsection there shall be inserted the following subsection –

"(1A) The diseases to which this subsection applies are –

(a) enteric fever (including typhoid and paratyphoid fevers);

(b) dysentery;

(c) diphtheria;

(d) scarlet fever;

(e) acute inflammation of the throat;

(f) gastro-enteritis; and

(g) undulant fever."

The Food and Environment Protection Act 1985 (c 48)

29. In section 24(1) of the Food and Environment Protection Act 1985 (interpretation) –

Appendix

(a) in the definition of "designated incident", for the words "designated incident" there shall be substituted the words "designated circumstances";

(b) the definition of "escape" shall cease to have effect; and

(c) for the definition of "food" there shall be substituted –

" 'food' has the same meaning as in the Food Safety Act 1990."

30. In section 25 of that Act (Northern Ireland) after subsection (4) there shall be inserted the following subsection –

"(4A) Section 24(1) above shall have effect in relation to Northern Ireland as if for the definition of 'food' there were substituted the following definition –

' "food" has the meaning assigned to it by Article 2(2) of the Food (Northern Ireland) Order 1989, except that it includes water which is bottled or is an ingredient of food'."

The Local Government Act 1985 (c 51)

31. In paragraph 15 of Schedule 8 to the Local Government Act 1985 (trading standards and related functions) –

(a) sub-paragraph (2) shall cease to have effect; and

(b) at the end of sub-paragraph (6) there shall be added the words "or section 5(1) of the Food Safety Act 1990".

The Weights and Measures Act 1985 (c 72)

32. In section 38 of the Weights and Measures Act 1985 (special powers of inspectors), subsection (4) (exclusion for milk) shall cease to have effect.

33. In section 93 of that Act (powers under other Acts with respect to marking of food) for the words "Food Act 1984" there shall be substituted the words "Food Safety Act 1990".

34. In section 94(1) of that Act (interpretation), in the definition of "drugs" and "food" for the words "Food Act 1984, or, in Scotland, the Food and Drugs (Scotland) Act 1956" there shall be substituted the words "Food Safety Act 1990".

The Agriculture Act 1986 (c 49)

35. In section 1(6) of the Agriculture Act 1986 (provision of agricultural goods and services), in the definition of "food", for the words, "Food Act 1984", there shall be substituted "Food Safety Act 1990".

The National Health Service (Amendment) Act 1986 (c 66)

36. – (1) In subsection (2) of section 1 of the National Health Service (Amendment) Act 1986 (application of food legislation to health authorities and health service premises) –

(a) for the words "appropriate authority" there shall be substituted the word "Ministers"; and

(b) for the word "authority" there shall be substituted the word "Ministers".

(2) For subsection (7) of that section there shall be substituted –

"(7) In this section –
'the Ministers' has the same meaning as in the Food Safety Act 1990;
'the food legislation' means the Food Safety Act 1990 and any regulations or orders made (or having effect as if made) under it;
'health authority' –

(a) as respects England and Wales, has the meaning assigned to it by section 128 of the 1977 Act; and

(b) as respects Scotland, means a Health Board constituted under section 2 of the 1978 Act, the Common Services Agency constituted under section 10 of that Act or a State Hospital Management Committee constituted under section 91 of the Mental Health (Scotland) Act 1984."

The Consumer Protection Act 1987 (c 43)

37. In section 19(1) of the Consumer Protection Act 1987 (interpretation of Part II), in the definition of "food" for the words "Food Act 1984" there shall be substituted "Food Safety Act 1990".

The Road Traffic Offenders Act 1988 (c 53)

38. In section 16(7) of the Road Traffic Offenders Act 1988 (meaning of "authorised analyst" in relation to proceedings under Act), for the words "section 76 of the Food Act 1984, or section 27 of the Food and Drugs (Scotland) Act 1956" there shall be substituted the words "section 27 of the Food Safety Act 1990".

SCHEDULE 4
Transitional Provisions and Savings

Ships and aircraft

1. In relation to any time before the commencement of the first order under section 1(3) of this Act –

(a) any ship which is a home-going ship within the meaning of section 132 of the 1984 Act or section 58 of the 1956 Act (interpretation) shall be regarded as premises for the purposes of this Act; and

(b) the powers of entry conferred by section 32 of this Act shall include the right to enter any ship or aircraft for the purpose of ascertaining whether there is in the ship or aircraft any food imported as part of the cargo in contravention of the provisions of regulations made under Part II of this Act;

and in this Act as it applies by virtue of this paragraph "occupier", in relation to any ship or aircraft, means the master, commander or other person in charge of the ship or aircraft.

Regulations under the 1984 Act

2. – (1) In so far as any existing regulations made, or having effect as if made, under any provision of the 1984 Act specified in the first column of Table A below have effect in relation to England and Wales, they shall have effect, after the commencement of the relevant repeal, as if made under the provisions of this Act specified in relation to that provision as in the second column of that Table, or such of those provisions as are applicable.

(2) In this paragraph and paragraphs 3 and 4 below "existing regulations" means –

(a) any regulations made, or having effect as if made, under a provision repealed by this Act; and

(b) any orders having effect as if made under such regulations,

which are in force immediately before the coming into force of that repeal; and references to the commencement of the relevant repeal shall be construed accordingly.

TABLE A

Provision of the 1984 Act	Provision of this Act
section 4 (composition etc. of food)	sections 16(1)(a), (c) and (f) and (3) and 17(1)
section 7 (describing food)	section 16(1)(e)
section 13 (food hygiene)	section 16(1)(b), (c), (d) and (f), (2) and (3)
section 33 (milk and dairies)	section 16(1)(b), (c), (d) and (f), (2) and (3)
section 34 (registration), so far as relating to dairies or dairy farms	section 19
section 38 (milk: special designations)	section 18(2)
section 73(2) (qualifications of officers)	section 5(6)
section 76(2) (public analysts)	section 27(2)
section 79(5) (form of certificate)	section 49(2)
section 119 (Community provisions)	section 17(2)

Regulations under the 1956 Act

3. Any existing regulations made, or having effect as if made, under any provision of the 1956 Act specified in the first column of Table B below shall have effect, after the commencement of the relevant appeal, as if made under the provisions of this Act specified in relation to that provision in the second column of that Table, or such of those provisions as are applicable.

TABLE B

Provision of the 1956 Act	Provision of this Act
section 4 (composition etc. of food)	sections 16(1)(a), (c) and (f) and (3) and 17(1)
section 7 (describing food)	section 16(1)(e)
section 13 (food hygiene)	sections 5(6) and 16(1)(b), (c), (d) and (f), (2) and (3)
section 16(2) (regulations as to milk)	section 18(2)
section 27(2) (public analysts)	section 27(2)
section 29(3) (form of certificate)	section 49(2)
section 56A (Community provisions)	section 17(2)

Other regulations

4. In so far as any existing regulations made under section 1 of the Importation of Milk Act 1983 have effect in relation to Great Britain, they shall have effect, after the commencement of the relevant repeal, as if made under section 18(1)(b) of this Act.

Orders with respect to milk in Scotland

5. – (1) Any existing order made under section 12(2) of the Milk and Dairies (Scotland) Act 1914 (orders with respect to milk) shall have effect, after the commencement of the relevant repeal, as if it were regulations made under section 16(1)(b), (d) and (f) and (2) of this Act.

(2) Any existing order made under section 3 of the Milk and Dairies (Amendment) Act 1922 (sale of milk under special designations) shall have effect, after the commencement of the relevant repeal, as if it were regulations made under section 18(2) of this Act.

(3) In this paragraph "existing order" means any order made under a provision repealed by this Act which is in force immediately before the coming into force of that repeal; and references to the commencement of the relevant repeal shall be construed accordingly.

Disqualification orders

6. The repeal by this Act of section 14 of the 1984 Act (court's power to disqualify caterers) shall not have effect as respects any order made, or having effect as if made, under that section which is in force immediately before the commencement of that repeal.

Food hygiene byelaws

7. – (1) The repeal by this Act of section 15 of the 1984 Act (byelaws as to food)

shall not have effect as respects any byelaws made, or having effect as if made, under that section which are in force immediately before the commencement of that repeal.

(2) In so far as any such byelaws conflict with any regulations made, or having effect as if made, under Part II of this Act, the regulations shall prevail.

Closure orders

8. The repeal by this Act of section 21 of the 1984 Act or section 1 of the Control of Food Premises (Scotland) Act 1977 (closure orders) shall not have effect as respects any order made, or having effect as if made, under that section which is in force immediately before the commencement of that repeal.

SCHEDULE 5
Repeals

Chapter	Short title	Extent of repeal
1914 c.46.	The Milk and Dairies (Scotland) Act 1914.	The whole Act.
1922 c.54.	The Milk and Dairies (Amendment) Act 1922.	The whole Act.
1934 c.51.	The Milk Act 1934.	The whole Act.
1949 c.34.	The Milk (Special Designations) Act 1949.	The whole Act.
1956 c.30.	The Food and Drugs (Scotland) Act 1956.	The whole Act.
1963 c.33.	The London Government Act 1963.	Section 54(1).
1967 c.22.	The Agriculture Act 1967.	In section 7(3), the words from "and, without prejudice" to the end.
1967 c.50.	The Farm and Garden Chemicals Act 1967.	In section 4(7)(c), the words from "for the reference" to "1956".
1968 c.29.	The Trade Descriptions Act 1968.	In section 22(2), the paragraph beginning with the words "In this subsection".
1968 c.67.	The Medicines Act 1968.	In section 132 (1), the definition of "food and drugs authority". In Schedule 5, paragraph 17.
1968 c.73.	The Transport Act 1968.	In Schedule 16, in paragraph 7(2), paragraphs (d) and (e).

Chapter	Short title	Extent of repeal
1971 c.62.	The Tribunals and Inquiries Act 1971.	In Schedule 1, paragraphs 15 and 40.
1972 c.66.	The Agriculture (Miscellaneous Provisions) Act 1972.	Section 4(3).
1972 c.68.	The European Communities Act 1972.	In Schedule 4, paragraph 3(2)(c).
1976 c.77.	The Weights and Measures etc. Act 1976.	In section 12(9)(c), the words "the 1956 Act or".
1977 c.28.	The Control of Food Premises (Scotland) Act 1977.	The whole Act.
1983 c.37.	The Importation of Milk Act 1983.	The whole Act.
1984 c.30.	The Food Act 1984.	Parts I and II. In section 51(2), the word "market". In section 53, in subsection (1) the words "and in respect of the weighing and measuring of articles and vehicles", and in subsection (3)(b) the words "in respect of the weighing of vehicles, or as the case may be." Section 57(1). Section 58. In section 61, the words from "and this Part" to the end. Part IV. Sections 70 to 92. In section 93, in subsection (2), paragraphs (b) to (d) and, in subsection (3), paragraphs (a) to (e) and (h) to (l). In section 94, subsection (1) except as regards offences under Part III of the Act, and subsection (2). In section 95, subsections (2) to (8). Sections 96 to 109. Sections 111 to 120. In section 121, subsections (2) and (3). Sections 122 to 131.

Chapter	Short title	Extent of repeal
		In section 132, subsection (1) except the words "In this Act, unless the context otherwise requires" and the definitions of "animal" and "the Minister". Sections 133 and 134. In section 136, in subsection (2), paragraphs (b) and (c). Schedules 1 to 11.
1985 c.48.	The Food and Environment Protection Act 1985.	In section 1(2), the definition of "escape". In section 24(1), the definition of "escape".
1985 c. 51.	The Local Government Act 1985.	In Schedule 8, paragraph 15(2).
1985 c.72.	The Weights and Measures Act 1985.	Section 38(4).

Index

Index

Index